Migration didn't erase my identity
It rewrote n

THE BROKEN COMPASS

THE BROKEN COMPASS

When Direction is Lost but Hope Remains

By Yousuf Mohammed
With Malick Mahmood

Disclaimer

This book is a work of non-fiction based on the personal experiences, observations, and perspectives of the author at the time of writing. It reflects the author's understanding of events, people, and socio-political conditions encountered during journey.

While every effort has been made to ensure accuracy, the ever-evolving nature of international politics, migration policies, and social realities means that some information may become outdated or interpreted differently over time.

Henceforth, the views expressed herein are those of the author and do not necessarily reflect those of any affiliated organizations, individuals, or entities. The author and co-author have taken reasonable care to verify the information presented; however, they make no representations or warranties of any kind, express or implied, regarding the completeness, accuracy, reliability, or suitability of the content for any purpose.

This publication is provided "as is." The author and co-author shall not be held liable for any direct, indirect, incidental, consequential, or punitive damages arising out of the use, misuse, or interpretation of the information contained within. Readers are encouraged to seek professional advice or conduct independent research when needed.

This book is not intended to promote or criticize any political stance or nation. It is, above all, a human story—a personal account of survival, loss, hope, and the pursuit of dignity.

All Rights Reserved

No part of this book may be reproduced, stored in a retrieval system, or transmitted in any form or by any means—electronic, mechanical, photocopying, recording, or otherwise—without the prior written permission of the author, except in the case of brief quotations used in reviews or scholarly articles.

Copyright © 2016 Yousuf Mohammed

Yousuf Mohammed has asserted his right under the Copyright, Designs and Patent Act, 1988, to be identified as the author of this work.

The Broken Compass | When Direction is Lost but Hope Remains is a work of non-fiction. Nonetheless, some names have been changed in order to disguise identities. Any resulting resemblance to persons living or dead is entirely coincidental and unintentional.

This story was first published by Yousuf Mohammed with Malick Mahmood on Amazon KDP in 2017 under the title "Second Chance | A Refugee Journey from Somalia to Germany."

Cover by: Malick Mahmood

For Enquiries:

Yousuf Mohammed:
yussuf.Mohammed@gmail.com

Malick Mahmood:
mahmoodmalick@gmail.com

Dedication

If words could feel the anguish
they describe,
they would refuse to exist.
These pages would fall silent—
blank—because
such sorrow would kill
the words themselves, and they would be buried forever
beneath the sands of the Sahara or the depths
of the Mediterranean Sea.
Dedicated to all those
who began this journey,
but never reached the other side.
This story is their voice—

---

the voice of the voiceless.

TABLE OF CONTENTS

Preface 9
Foreword 11
Mohammed | Kismayo - Somalia 15
Crossroads 25
Ocean Stars 39
Aaliyah 49
Kismayo to Addis Ababa, Ethiopia 63
Addis Ababa to Khartoum, Sudan 79
Khartoum to Middle of Nowhere 107
Sahara Desert to Sabha, Libya 135
Sabha to Tripoli 161
Across the Mediterranean 183
Italy to Munich, Germany 193
Conclusion 213
Glossary of Terms & Phrases 217
About Yousuf Mohammed 221
About Malick Mahmood 223

Preface

The hundred days it took me to reach Germany felt like a hundred lifetimes. What I lived through during that journey is almost beyond imagination. There's a saying: "Pain that doesn't kill you makes you stronger." If that's true, then I must be strong. I built my strength by running six kilometers nearly every day—but even that was not enough. It still took every ounce of mental and physical courage I had to recount this story.

I came close to death more than once.

Once, while escaping from a private prison in Libya. And once more—perhaps the most haunting of all—when I drifted across the Mediterranean in a fragile plastic boat, packed with ninety others. Among us were four pregnant women. One of them was carrying the child of a smuggler who had raped her.

In the desert, the girls were always the most vulnerable. The traffickers, without shame or mercy, would drag them into tents while mocking us men with their cruelty. Rape wasn't hidden—it was part of the power they wielded.

Those who trafficked us had long since sold their souls. They cared for nothing but money—and they would do anything, demand anything, and break anyone to get it.

I feel compelled to tell this story for two reasons.

First, for those who never made it. I want to share the dreams they carried—dreams that died somewhere between the sand dunes of the Sahara and the depths of the Mediterranean. Most of them were barely nineteen. Their lives, like candles in the wind, were extinguished far too soon.

Second, I want to respond to those in Europe who say, "Refugees are draining our resources." These people don't know what it cost us to stand here, alive. We didn't simply walk through a border. We crawled through fire. We survived things that words can never fully capture. Freedom has a price—and many of us paid it with our bodies, our innocence, our loved ones.

I believe that no matter how much I may earn in life, no matter how much success I find—it will never equal the price I paid to get here. Yes, I'm grateful for the peace Europe has given me. But if I had known back then — standing on Somali soil — what horrors I would face on the road ahead, I would never have taken the first step.

Finally, I must thank my friend and brother, Malick Mahmood. Without his skill, empathy, and perseverance, this story might never have found its voice. This Pakistani brother stood by me, listened with his heart, and spent three tireless years shaping my memories into these pages—with no thought of personal gain. For that, I will always be grateful.

Yousuf Mohammed

Foreword

I've always loved stories—reading them, writing them—whether they're fiction or grounded in truth. But nothing could have prepared me for the raw, harrowing reality of Yousuf's story. My heart aches for the countless souls around the world who are forced to make desperate choices in pursuit of a future—a future that promises not luxury, but dignity. After reading this story, I believe you'll feel the same.

Yousuf's journey reminds us of the quiet blessings we so often overlook: A glass of clean water; A handful of fresh fruit or vegetables; A sliver of shade under a blazing sun; A blanket to ward off the night's chill. Things we treat as ordinary—yet for many, they are a matter of life and death.

This is more than a refugee's story. It is a mirror held up to humanity, revealing the grotesque face of greed and the depths of depravity some humans descend into when compassion is stripped away.

Once, during one of our interviews, I asked Yousuf a question that stayed with me: "If you were given a second chance, would you take the same journey again?"

Without hesitation, he said no.

Naturally, I followed up— "Then what would you have done instead, back in Somalia?"

His answer shook me. He told me the soil in Somalia is very fertile—so rich that it doesn't even need fertilizer. Just seeds. One handful of seeds, he said, could have grown enough food to feed him. If he had simply had enough to eat, he would never have left.

It was a revelation. One that international organizations and policymakers must listen to: If you truly want to make a difference, don't just send aid—send seeds, tools, irrigation systems, and generators to farmers. Empower the people where they are, so they never have to become refugees.

This story also reveals something deeper within the human psyche. It shows how prolonged suffering can strip away emotions, values, and even the most basic ethics—until all that remains will be the primal will to survive. In a desert where the sun burns by day and the cold bites by night, survival becomes the only law.

Yousuf speaks of a girl named Ayesha—he met her in the Sahara, both of them captives of human traffickers. I once asked him, cautiously, if he had felt any affection for her. His response was nothing like what I expected.

In a place where humanity was reduced to silence, even love had no space to bloom.

I wish there were a way to stop people from embarking on this horrific journey. Yet, even knowing the monstrous challenges ahead, thousands of men and women—some as young as sixteen, others as old as fifty or more—continue to walk the same path. Not because they want to, but because they feel they have no other choice.

This story is a cry from that path.

It is a voice rising from the silence.

And I hope it reaches those who can still make a difference.

Malick Mahmood

Due to a severe shortage of ambulances in Somalia, most people rely on taxis or private cars to transport the wounded to hospitals. A speeding vehicle blaring its horn nonstop was often a sign of such an emergency.

15
Mohammed | Kismayo - Somalia

I had already finished my *Dhuhr* prayer, but my friends were still engaged in theirs. Suddenly, I heard a familiar sound in the distance—Ghoowww Ghooowww—a vehicle horn blaring continuously.

Faulty horns often produce an odd, unsettling noise. But the sound soon faded, signaling that the vehicle had arrived at the hospital.

Due to a severe shortage of ambulances in Somalia, most people rely on taxis or private cars to transport the wounded—or the dead —to hospitals.

A speeding vehicle blaring its horn nonstop was often a sign of such an emergency.

The constant overuse of horns had worn them down, distorting their sound into something far more haunting than the ever-present echo of gunfire.

As I stepped out of the mosque, leaving my friends behind, a familiar question crossed my mind: "Who will it be this time?"

That dreadful sound always drew me toward the hospital—almost instinctively—as if I were a doctor or a nurse, though I was neither. But with a chronic shortage of medical staff, I did whatever I could: helping carry the wounded to the wards or the dead to the mortuary.

Sometimes, I recognized the victim. In those times, I would rush to their home to inform the family—so they could either offer support to their loved one or collect their body.

On my way to the hospital that day, I came across a man speaking about a shooting that had occurred about an hour earlier. I joined a small crowd gathered around him, listening intently. "He got caught in the crossfire," the man said. "A bullet hit his leg. They rushed him to the hospital—he was bleeding heavily."

In our region, it was common for men to carry AK-47s or similar weapons openly. Even boys as young as nine or ten often carried loaded machine guns. Many of them were recruited by the militant group *Al-Shabab* and proudly referred to themselves as *Al-Jihadi*.

Armed clashes between rival factions had become a grim part of daily life in Somalia. These battles could erupt between tribal or terrorist militias and government forces—or simply between men of feuding tribes. Sometimes, even a minor political disagreement or personal quarrel was enough to spark gunfire. Tragically, the majority of victims in such incidents were innocent bystanders. Their deaths were often dismissed as just another "stray bullet" case. Yet, stray bullets have claimed thousands of lives in Somalia.

I arrived at the restaurant where, just an hour earlier, I had been having tea with my friends. It was as busy as ever. A few elderly men now occupied the spot where we had been sitting. I remembered that my friend Mohammed had left early and hadn't joined us for prayers. The others—Ahmed, Razzaq, and Saeed—had stayed until we heard the *adhan* calling us to the mosque. It was during those prayers that I first heard the car horn blaring nonstop.

In Kismayo, restaurants and teashops are popular gathering spots—especially for older men. They often sit for hours, sipping tea cup after cup, usually deep in political discussions. But when that familiar, continuous horn sounds, conversations stop. Everyone wants to know what happened and who the victim is. That day was no different. The talk was all about the shooting and the young man who had been hit. I knew most of it was just speculation.

It usually took me about ten minutes of brisk walking to reach the hospital from the mosque.

As I got closer, I could already picture the scene—people pulling a wounded, bleeding body out of a car. Drivers sometimes shouted in frustration at the sight of blood soaking their seats.

When I finally arrived, a crowd had gathered at the hospital entrance. I knew getting inside wouldn't be easy.

Our hospital was nothing like those in the developed world. It was a small house, hastily converted into a makeshift facility with a few beds, chairs, and desks—hardly worthy of being called a hospital. It lacked even the most basic medicines, including those needed to stop bleeding.

I had seen people bleed to death more than once. One of those times, it was a police officer. As usual, I rushed to the hospital when I heard the horn. When I arrived, I saw people carrying his body toward the mortuary. As I looked at him closely, I noticed his lips moving. "He's still alive! He's moving!" I shouted. The men immediately lowered the stretcher and saw for themselves. They turned back and wheeled him into the treatment room. In a panic, they pushed the stretcher next to the sink and tilted his head into it so the blood wouldn't spill onto the floor. I stood silently at the door, watching his blood pour into the sink and disappear down the drain. His family and friends had rushed out to find a doctor, but by the time they returned, it was too late. The police officer was dead.

Our hospital wasn't busy treating patients—it was busy letting them die.

The police officer wasn't the only one. Another time, I watched a thirteen-year-old girl bleed to death. She lay on a stretcher, her face pale and growing paler, and I could see death slowly settling in her eyes. She had been part of a group of children throwing rocks at each other. One of the rocks apparently struck someone's house. The homeowner called the police, and the children were arrested and locked in a single cell. Inside, they continued to argue and fight, making noise and banging on the door. An officer came to the cell, pulled out his gun, pointed it through a hole in the door, and while ordering them to be quiet, fired a shot. The bullet struck the girl in the thigh. She was rushed to the hospital—and that's where I saw her. The doctors had no supplies to stop the bleeding. Her family stood by helplessly as she slipped away, inch by inch, her life draining out. She was just a child, barely at the threshold of life—and now she was gone.

Those moments haunted me. I kept asking myself: What if it were me bleeding on that stretcher, or into that sink? Even now, the memory makes me tremble.

"Who was it?" someone behind me asked. I had the same question. "It was a young boy. His name was Mohammed," a man in front of me replied. The name Mohammed is so common in Islamic countries that it didn't strike me as unusual—or even make me think of my friend Mohammed, who had been with me just a few hours earlier.

I wanted to go inside and see for myself, to make sure, but the entrance was blocked by a large crowd. Men were guarding the doorway, and if they had seen me, they wouldn't have let me through.

Somehow, I managed to slip past them unnoticed.

The main entrance opened into a short hallway—no reception desk, no hospital staff to guide anyone, just chaos. If I wanted answers, I had to get to the treatment room. Its door opened and closed constantly as people came and went. Sometimes it stayed ajar, giving quick, flickering glimpses of what was happening inside.

I pushed my way forward and finally reached the front of the crowd. There, I recognized a few neighborhood boys I used to play football with. They saw me too. "Who is it?" I asked loudly. "It's Mohammed, our friend," one of them replied.

I froze. For a moment, I couldn't believe it. "Are you sure?" I asked again, hoping I had misheard.

But they nodded. It was indeed Mohammed.

I pushed closer to one of the boys. "What happened?" I asked. He repeated the same story I had heard earlier—the one about the crossfire, the bullet to the leg, the heavy bleeding.

We moved around together, trying to learn more, but no one paid attention to us. We were just kids—too young to be noticed, too powerless to get answers. All I knew was that my friend was in that room, bleeding to death—and I couldn't get to him.

It was hard to believe that my friend—who had been laughing and talking with us just a few hours earlier—was now fighting for his life. And all I could do was pray.

A wave of emotions crashed over me: anger, helplessness, inadequacy, and grief.

I was angry with all of my friends—Ahmed, Saeed, Razzaq, and even Mohammed—because they had ignored my pleas to leave Somalia. I had warned them, again and again, but they never took me seriously. This time, the stray bullet had found Mohammed.

I was furious at everyone who carried a weapon. Couldn't they see that Somalia was slowly bleeding to death? Wasn't it a basic human right to live—and to let others live—in peace?

The international organizations that claimed to defend human rights had failed us completely.

And our own political system? It was hopeless. For people like us—young, ordinary, and powerless—there was no future here.

I made myself a promise: "Once Mohammed recovers, I will convince him to leave Somalia with me."

Tears streamed down my face as I stood silently in the hospital corridor, waiting for the door to the treatment room to open.

I saw some of Mohammed's family at the front of the crowd. I wanted to speak to them, but stopped myself when I noticed the shock etched on their faces. Still, they held onto hope, clinging to the idea that the wound—just a bullet to the thigh—wasn't life-threatening.

"He's going to be okay," one of them said, trying to sound confident. I wanted to believe them. I truly did. But I had seen too much. I remembered the others who had gone into that room, never to walk out again.

When the treatment room door finally opened, I surged forward, desperate for a glimpse of my friend. But I wasn't family—they stopped me.

About thirty minutes later, the hospital staff wheeled Mohammed out on a stretcher. "He's dead," they announced, coldly, without the slightest trace of compassion.

His family broke down.

They cried out, clinging to each other, asking how it could be. How could he die from a wound to the leg?

No one from the hospital offered an explanation. No comfort. No apology. Just the same brutal answer, repeated:

He's dead. Take him home.

But I knew the truth—Mohammed wasn't killed by the bullet. He was killed by the blood he lost and the care he never received.

I had never seen anyone come out of that treatment room alive. Mohammed was no exception.

We carried his body out of the hospital.

His family walked beside us, drained and broken, bearing the weight of their seventeen-year-old son on their shoulders—and the burden of a nation that could not protect its children.

Mohammed didn't belong to a strong tribe or powerful group. That meant there would be no justice for his murder—none at all.

In Somalia, justice was a privilege reserved for the powerful.

It wasn't the police or the courts that decided such matters; it was the tribal chiefs who held authority over guilt, innocence, and punishment.

If the victim's tribe was strong enough, they could demand blood money—or even exact revenge. In those cases, the accused would be blindfolded, tied to a tree, and the victim's family would be handed a gun. One by one, they would shoot the offender until it was done. And that would be the end of it. The matter would be considered settled.

But for those from weaker tribes—like Mohammed's—there was only silence. Their families knew better than to demand justice. They knew that raising their voices could lead to more bloodshed.

In a land ruled not by law but by might, asking for justice could be more dangerous than letting the matter go.

It wasn't a country anymore. It was a jungle, and survival belonged to the strongest.

Later that same day, after the *Asr* prayer, we offered *Janaza* for Mohammed. Before *Maghreb*, we buried him. I walked away from the graveyard with a heavy heart, grieving the friend I would never see again.

Mohammed had been kindhearted—a gentle soul who never deserved such a brutal end. Like all of us, he dreamed of one day giving his family a life of peace and dignity.

"He couldn't give his family a peace," I told my friends quietly as we walked, "but at least now he is at peace."

In Somalia, It wasn't the police or the courts that decided matters between two rival parties; it was, instead the tribal chiefs who held authority over guilt, innocence, and punishment

But peace was something Somalia never gave its people. Neither the Somali governments nor the countless international humanitarian organizations ever provided the most basic medical care for us. Our hospitals were broken, our systems failed, and our future felt like a road to nowhere.

Mohammed's death forced me to look at my surroundings with new eyes. Everything looked darker. I couldn't help but dream of another place—somewhere far from the gunfire, somewhere safe, where I could protect my family from this endless cycle of violence and loss. A place where my parents wouldn't be left to die in a hallway if they ever fell sick.

But nothing changed after Mohammed died. Not in Somalia, and not in Kismayo. Every day, we still heard the chilling stutter of gunfire, often followed by the haunting, defective blare of a car horn.

Ghoowww... Ghoowww...

Each time I heard it, I ran.

And each time, I asked myself the same question:

"Who will it be this time?"

25
Crossroads

It had only been a few days since Mohammed's death, but we didn't have the luxury of prolonged mourning. We had no choice but to push on, burying our grief, just to survive. But even in the midst of our struggles, questions lingered:

Did our lives matter?

Did we have a future in Somalia?

Was there any hope for a life worth living?

None of these questions had good answers—each one led only to death.

The civil war had obliterated our economy and shattered our lives. Our markets, our businesses, our sense of peace—everything was lost. Hunger and death now walked the streets. Whether it came from a bullet or from starvation, both killed. We longed for serenity, for a break from the constant fight for survival, but peace was a distant dream. We were no longer safe anywhere—not on the streets, and not even in our own homes. Every moment felt like a battle, and every day was another fight to live.

Conditions in Somalia, and in my hometown of Kismayo, continued to worsen. But this was the world I had been born into; it was all I had ever known. I had never witnessed a real government or experienced any semblance of law and order. Politics held no appeal for me. They had brought only chaos, poverty, and despair. Each day, we heard about more killings—educators, doctors, engineers, and even the few honest politicians were targeted. It felt like genocide, slowly tearing our country apart.

The high-ranking officials and ministers, those who could have made a difference, were indifferent. They were too busy building their own empires.

It was common for someone from a powerful tribe to stand up, don a suit, and declare himself the president of a state—often within another state. At the same time, another would rise up, claiming control over a different region, declaring his own state. These so-called presidents would fill their administrations with loyalists from their own tribes, ignoring the needs of the people. The politicians and state presidents of Somalia were largely power-hungry individuals who cared only for their own interests. Their energy was spent on fighting each other, not on helping the people. The states were small, fragmented territories. Back when we were children, we could travel freely between them—playing football in one state, offering prayers in another. But now, the political boundaries were drawn with blood, and anyone who dared to cross them could be shot on sight.

Everywhere, it was a constant struggle for power—an endless competition to gain more and more.

It wasn't just the presidents and their supporters grabbing for control. *Al-Shabab* was a major player in this power game, and their influence wasn't confined to any one region or state. They spread far and wide, actively recruiting young men to join their militant group. Their leaders and loyal followers traveled across the country, making speeches that urged people to join them: "We will provide you with weapons to protect your family; we will give you food for your family."

Widespread unemployment, poverty, and physical insecurity left many vulnerable to Al-Shabab's promises, allowing them to build their own army.

Politics in Somalia grew ever more hopeless and confusing. There were some presidents who pledged allegiance to Al-Shabab, while others stood against them.

Those who opposed Al-Shabab would sometimes ally with the Somali Central Government, making it yet another player in this deadly power struggle. The Somali army, alongside its allied presidents, fought Al-Shabab and their own set of allies.

It seemed as though every man in Somalia was trying to kill the other. In their ignorance and arrogance, our rulers had created a society where almost everyone carried a weapon. Gangs of heavily armed thugs roamed freely, looting, raping, and committing every imaginable crime against anyone they encountered.

"Things weren't always like this," my mom would often say. She was an educated woman, a teacher, and she knew Somalia's history well. When she spoke of the past, it felt like a distant dream, almost like a fantasy to my friends and me. She told us of a time when our land was fertile, where crops thrived and livestock were healthy. There were schools, colleges, and hospitals. But most importantly, there was law—order.

"I wish we had the Somalia you remember," I would say to her whenever she shared those memories of a better time.

Somalia gained its independence in 1960, with the unification of *British Somaliland* and *Italian Somaliland*. AbdiRashid Ali Sharmarke became our first prime minister and later our president from 1967 to 1969. Under his leadership, Somalia flourished in education, agriculture, and industry.

In 1964, when Ethiopia invaded Somalia, a reporter asked Prime Minister Sharmarke how his government could manage both elections and the war with Ethiopia at the same time.

His response was unforgettable: "We will fight with one hand and hold elections with the other."

The people of Somalia adored him, and under his guidance, Somalia had the potential to become a different country altogether.

In 1964, when Ethiopia invaded Somalia, a reporter asked Sharmarke how his government could manage both elections and the war at the same time. "We will fight with one hand and hold elections with the other," He responded.

Image Credits: Portrait of President of Somalia Abdirashid Ali Shermarke By Government of Somalia - Puntland News 24.

But then tragedy struck. He was assassinated by one of his own bodyguards, and that act irrevocably changed the course of our history.

Following the assassination of President Sharmarke on October 15, 1969, the military seized control. Just a day after his funeral, on October 21, Major General Mohammed Siad Barre led a bloodless coup and assumed power without opposition. Though no blood was shed that day, the takeover would plunge Somalia into decades of endless conflict.

"Everyone wanted to rule," my mother would say, as she explained how the fall of Barre's regime in 1990 ignited a never-ending insurgency. "Some called it a civil war, others a political revolution. Now it's sometimes called *Jihad*. But to me," she would say with sorrow in her voice, "it's genocide—the mass murder of Somalians."

The so-called revolution that ended Barre's dictatorship quickly descended into civil war, claiming hundreds of thousands of lives and displacing millions. Those millions, still internally displaced, now live in tents with no protection from theft, murder, or rape. The worst consequence of the conflict was famine. An estimated 300,000 to 400,000 people starved to death in just one decade. "I've heard gunshots and rockets for nearly forty years now. Everything is destroyed," my mother would say, her eyes filled with tears.

We Somalians are resilient and fiercely independent. Even in the darkest times, we pretend everything is normal and carry on with our lives. But the civil war had completely transformed Somalia, and it would take divine intervention to repair what had been broken.

Image Credits: Military portrait of Major General Mohamed Siad Barre By Government of Somalia

Day after Sharmarke funeral, on October 21, Major General Mohammed Siad Barre led a bloodless coup and assumed power. Though no blood was shed that day, the takeover plunged Somalia into decades of endless conflict.

I became consumed with worry for my parents and my family. They weren't safe in Kismayo—no one was safe anywhere in Somalia. Anything could happen to anyone, at any time. I often discussed this with my friends.

"Do we not have the right to live in peace and harmony?" I would ask.

"I want to get out of here and live somewhere I can find peace and live a good, responsible life," my friend Ahmed would say.

I felt exactly the same. Like him, I dreamed of leaving. We both wanted to support our families—but we knew we couldn't do it in Somalia.

Another major socio-political shift occurred in 2004, when the Islamic *Sharia* court took control of our region. A group of influential tribal chiefs allied themselves with Al-Shabab and several Sharia court judges to establish yet another self-declared government to rule Kismayo.

Al-Shabab thugs were everywhere. They moved freely through the markets, collecting taxes from businesses and farmers as if they were a legitimate authority. On the streets, they claimed to be enforcing the law, but in truth, they were the ones violating it.

Their presence was suffocating. Their spies lurked in every corner, listening to conversations, watching every move. Speaking out against them was dangerous—people disappeared, or worse, were killed for merely expressing dissent against the so-called local government, the Al-Shabab government.

Keeping food on the table was a constant struggle for those of us who refused to join the lawlessness of Al-Shabab. I shared whatever small amounts I earned from odd jobs with my mother. As the eldest, it was my responsibility.

Despite everything, we never gave up football. We played almost every afternoon—it was our only escape. When we didn't have a real ball, we'd tie our socks together, stuff them with garbage, and shape them into something round. We kicked that makeshift ball across dusty fields like it was a prized possession.

I didn't know it then, but I would soon miss that ball made of socks more than I could have imagined.

I wanted to make my father proud, and I knew guns were not the way to do it. I needed to pursue something honorable—something that would make him stand tall and say, "Yousuf is my son, and I'm proud of him."

"You really think that great and dignified thing is to go to Europe?" my friend Razzaq once asked me.

I told him how Europe offered a chance to study, to work, and to live with freedom. "Europe gives you a shot at doing something meaningful with your life," I said.

"There are plenty who tried that and were never seen again. Their bodies still haven't been found," Razzaq argued.

I replied, "What killed our friend Mohammed? If he had left for Europe, maybe he'd still be alive today."

Razzaq and Saeed never shared my dream. They kept searching for something they could do here, in Somalia. But Ahmed—he was with me all the way. "I'll go with you when the time comes," he'd say, firmly and without hesitation.

Rumors of another battle began to spread. In restaurants and tea stalls, people whispered about an ultimate showdown—Al-Shabab on one side, and on the other, the united forces of Somalia, Kenya, and several African nations. Some even said NATO might get involved. I heard from many elders that our hometown, Kismayo, was going to be the final battleground.

Kismayo sits on the banks of the great Juba River where it meets the Indian Ocean. Its strategic position has made it Somalia's greatest port city and a hub of international trade for centuries.

In 2011, Al-Shabab had been pushed out of Mogadishu. By the end of 2012, Kismayo was their last stronghold, and they weren't going to give it up without a fight. Their militia leaders made that clear—loudly and often—during public gatherings and Friday sermons. "As a Muslim, you are obligated to fight them because they are infidels," they declared.

I found it all deeply confusing. The state-run radio in Mogadishu also claimed, "Somalia is at war against infidels." Yet both sides insisted they were true Muslims and accused the other of betrayal.

Al-Shabab knew what was coming. Their camps were buzzing with activity. They increased tolls on goods entering and leaving Kismayo and hiked taxes on farmers and nomads. That money funded their war against the government. They even launched their own radio broadcasts, filled with propaganda, to indoctrinate youth and recruit new fighters.

The government in Mogadishu knew that if they could take back Kismayo, it would strike a devastating blow to Al-Shabab—cutting off one of their most vital sources of funding.

Almost six months before I left Somalia in 2012, the stage was set for the final battle between the Somali government and Al-Shabab. I could sense what was coming. The impending war would kill or displace thousands.

Radio BBC reported that Al-Shabab had officially declared its alliance with *Al-Qaeda*.

Militia camps had sprung up around the outskirts of Kismayo, training new recruits. They offered food, money, and shelter—just enough to tempt desperate young men into picking up a gun. Soon, the only way to survive in Kismayo was to join Al-Shabab and become a killer.

Then one night in September 2012, we heard breaking news: African Union Forces had landed near Kismayo. "They are preparing to attack Al-Shabab," BBC reported.

Panic swept through the city. Thousands had already fled. Many more packed what little they could and prepared to leave. Children cried, women screamed, and the elderly stumbled behind the fleeing crowds, not knowing where they were going—only that they had to go.

But my mother refused to leave.

"I was born here, and I'll die here," she said. And so, my family stayed behind.

Then the attack came—by land, air, and sea. The fighting was brutal. Machine guns rattled day and night. Rockets exploded in the distance, shaking walls and hearts. We huddled together in fear, unsure if we would see the next morning.

In just a few days, Al-Shabab officially lost control of Kismayo and its port. But the war didn't end. It only changed form. The militia melted into the countryside, into the mountains, into hidden bases. Guerilla warfare began, and with it came a new wave of fear—ambushes, assassinations, bombings.

Then, like Al-Shabab before them, the Somali army began recruiting. They offered food, clothing, and shelter to attract young men. But the mission was the same: pick up a gun, and kill for your side.

I didn't join. Neither did my friends.

I have never held a gun—and I never want to. To kill another human being, you would need a sick mind and a cold heart. I never wanted to become that person.

The circumstances around me placed my life at a crossroads, and I had to choose a path. There were four choices.

Two involved staying and killing: join the military or join the militia. Both offered survival at the cost of humanity.

The other two options meant leaving my homeland to escape the war and bloodshed—but neither of those was easy either. One was to take our families to a UN refugee camp in Kenya, Ethiopia, or Uganda. At least there, we would be safe from bullets. But safety came with a different kind of suffering.

We had heard from elders at tea stalls and restaurants that those camps were hellish. People were treated like animals. There were no schools, no jobs—just barbed wire, hopelessness, and meals thrown over fences. A life without dignity. I knew my mother would never agree to live like that.

The fourth option was to travel to Europe.

It remained my first choice, even though it meant risking my life.

"People have died on the way, Yousuf," Razzaq warned me. "I've heard stories—refugees kidnapped in the middle of the Sahara. They take out their kidneys and organs to sell, then dump the bodies in the desert."

I understood his fear. But I also felt cornered.

"So what should we do?" I argued. "Join the militia? Or drag our families to those camps just to starve and be humiliated?"

"Yousuf is right," Ahmed said, as always backing me. "The only way out is to go to Europe."

"Through the valley of death," Razzaq muttered grimly.

"Razzaq, my brother," Ahmed responded quietly, "we already live in the valley of death."

I often shared what I had learned from Somali contacts who had made it to Germany. "They live in peace. Some are studying. Others have jobs. Just imagine—real schools, organized football, a life of dignity and opportunity."

I saw it in my mind so clearly it felt almost real. A new beginning.

Those who couldn't choose among the four options—the uncertain ones—stayed behind. Most couldn't afford the journey or couldn't bear its hardships. Many were from the older generation. They sat in the streets every day, chewing miraa, getting high, wasting away.

That was their escape. Sleep through the storm. Pretend none of it mattered.

We talked often about the journey, but never made a decision. Our debates ended the same way each time—someone sighed, and everyone quietly left for home. Life carried on in a strange and numb routine, even with death constantly watching from the shadows.

I wore #9 on my national jersey I still remember the pride I felt when I played for the Somalian National Team in the CECAFA Cup in 2011. That moment was nothing short of a dream come true.

# 39
Ocean Stars

When I was in Somalia, I spent much of my time worrying about the safety and well-being of my loved ones. Fear had become a constant companion. But in the midst of all that, there was one thing that always lifted my spirit—football.

Whether I was playing or just thinking about the game, football gave me a sense of purpose. It reminded me that there was more to life than just survival.

I still remember the pride I felt when I played for the Somalian National Team in the Council for East and Central Africa Football Associations (CECAFA) Cup in 2011. That moment was nothing short of a dream come true.

Our team was called the Ocean Stars, and indeed, I felt like a star. A proud Ocean Star. That jersey, those matches—they were more than sport. They were hope.

We played our first match against Burundi. The Tanzanian National Stadium was packed with spectators, most of them cheering for our opponents. The noise, the energy, the emotions—it was overwhelming.

I wore #9 on my national jersey. As we lined up and stood shoulder to shoulder, they played our national anthem. Even now, I can still hear it—like a whisper echoing from the past: *Soomaaliyeey toosoo, toosoo isku tiirsada ee. Hadba kiina taagdaranee, taageera waligiinee. Sharcigaa isku kiin tolayoo, luuqadaa tuwaaxid ahoo* (Somalis, wake up; rise and support one another. Stand by those who are weak among you—support them forever. The law has united you, and your language makes you one).

That anthem, *"Soomaaliyeey Toosoo"* (Somalis Wake Up), stirred something powerful in us. It remained our national anthem until August 2012, when *"Qolobaa Calankeed"* (Praise the Homeland) became the official anthem of the Federal Republic of Somalia. But to me, the old anthem still lives—etched into my heart from that unforgettable day.

Even that day in the Tanzanian National Stadium, I thought about my mother. She had supported me in every way she could, and it was because of her that I was there. She had been an excellent basketball player in her student days and always encouraged me to pursue football at a professional level.

I started playing football when I was just a kid—it quickly became the passion of my life. Most children in Somalia grow up with a football at their feet. It's often the only game we know. When I started, people would say, "Yousuf is fast." Their encouragement motivated me to dream bigger, to become a professional player.

Football is a wonderful game. It sharpens concentration and helps relieve stress. Most importantly, it creates deep and lasting friendships. When people come together to play, tribe, race, caste, and color lose all meaning. Football also teaches persistence in the face of adversity. I believe that it was our experience on the football field that helped my friends and me stay focused on the positive, even when life around us was collapsing.

Despite our deep love for the sport, Somalia hasn't performed well in international tournaments. The war has made proper training and preparation nearly impossible. But just showing up mattered.

During CECAFA 2011, one journalist wrote, "The Ocean Stars have come a long way this year to compete in CECAFA 2011. They've made it from the war-weary Horn of Africa country of Somalia. That in itself is a great achievement."

Al-Shabab viewed football as a satanic game. Mahmoud Amin, one of Somalia's greatest football players, was among the 35 people killed in a car explosion claimed by Al-Shabab. They declared that football was *haram* (forbidden) and threatened to punish anyone who dared to defy their beliefs. This deeply affected our football community. The passion we had for the game, the dreams we carried, were being overshadowed by fear. Football, once a unifying force, was now seen through a lens of danger and violence.

The second reason Somalia hasn't fared well in international tournaments is the lack of incentive for players. Football was often viewed as a foolish pursuit, something people would laugh at if you took it seriously. The rewards were too distant, and the environment too hostile. Those who dedicated themselves to football had to endure ridicule, poverty, and constant threats. For many, the risk outweighed the reward, and the dream of international glory seemed like an unreachable fantasy.

I watched as many talented players gave up hope of ever having a career in football. Some, as young as fifteen, turned to chewing miraa, while others not much older were already married with children. The harsh realities of life in Somalia had stolen their dreams, and football no longer seemed like a path worth following.

But I never stopped playing. My love for the game was unwavering. I didn't care about the money—or the lack of it. I didn't care about the challenges or the people who told me there was no future in football. I stayed focused, driven by a belief in myself and my passion.

I was lucky enough to earn a place on the Somalian national team. For someone like me, from a humble background with no high-status family or clan ties, this was no small feat. I didn't have influential connections to pave the way for me. But I was fast, and that caught the attention of the scouts. They had no choice but to take me.

Although I only played in one tournament, the experience was an honor that I'll cherish forever.

Being part of the Ocean Stars—the national football squad—was a dream come true.

Playing with the national team gave me more than just the chance to represent my country—it also gave me a glimpse into the inner workings of team management.

It became painfully clear that the team's leaders were less concerned about whether we won or lost, and more focused on the match fees they collected.

Each player received a match fee of US $350 from CECAFA, and the team managers were pocketing all those thousands of dollars for each match. On top of that, there were likely additional payments from sponsors.

It felt like our participation in CECAFA 2011 was not about playing the game or striving for victory, but about the money. We lost all three games in our pool, which led to our elimination from the tournament.

I knew we could have performed better if the management had done their job properly.

I couldn't stay silent.

I've always felt compelled to speak out, even when I know the consequences.

I raised my concerns, openly questioning how things were being handled.

I believe that if you see something wrong, you have an obligation to speak up. But as I soon learned, speaking the truth came with a heavy cost.

After CECAFA 2011, I was no longer selected for the national team. My outspokenness had cost me my place on the squad, a price I was willing to pay.

Twelve national teams from across Africa participated in the CECAFA tournament. We were placed in Group B, alongside top-level teams from Uganda, Burundi, and Zanzibar. It was a tough group by any standard.

Our first match was against Burundi, and we lost 4–1. The only goal we scored came from a penalty that I had created. It was a small personal victory in the midst of a demoralizing experience.

We left our hotel at 11:00 a.m. for the 2:00 p.m. kickoff. The travel itself was tiring, and around 1:00 p.m., they handed us lunch—plain rice and cheap soft drinks.

Yes, players can eat up to three hours before a match, but the meal needs to be light and nutritious, providing maximum energy without weighing you down. Ours was neither.

The problems didn't stop there. We were given low-quality sports shoes that became uncomfortably hot during play. Luckily, our first game was on grass. But we already knew the next match against Uganda would be on astroturf—and those shoes would burn on synthetic turf. To make matters worse, during the match, we were handed bottles of warm water while the Burundi players refreshed themselves with chilled energy drinks.

We didn't just lose to a more skilled team—we lost to a system that failed us at every level.

The Burundi team was organized, well-supported, and professionally equipped. We, on the other hand, had been set up to fail before we even stepped on the field.

Our second match was against another strong contender—Uganda.

Just like before, we were served rice and warm water before the game, and once again we entered the field with our stomachs full and our energy low. But despite everything stacked against us, we had made a decision: we would fight.

The stadium was packed, most of the crowd cheering for Uganda. But to everyone's surprise, we held them scoreless in the first half. We even came close to scoring ourselves.

We played with heart, with determination.

At halftime, our feet were burning from the synthetic turf, so we plunged them into buckets of ice-cold water. It gave temporary relief, but it couldn't restore the morale we were slowly losing. By the second half, exhaustion and frustration had caught up with us.

I played forward in that game. At one point, I tackled the ball and sprinted toward Uganda's goal. Four large defenders closed in on me. I looked to my left, then right, hoping for support—but my teammates were far behind, too exhausted to catch up.

I had no choice but to kick the ball out of bounds.

I was angry—angry at the poor management, the lack of planning, the way we were being treated.

My frustration affected my focus, and the coach pulled me out of the game.

Shortly afterward, Uganda scored.

Then another.

We lost 4–0—our second humiliating defeat.

The managers and coaches didn't seem to care. They weren't the ones out on the field, facing the crowd, wearing the national colors. But we were. And we were devastated. We had given it our all.

Our third and final match was against Zanzibar.

By then, our spirits were broken.

Nothing had changed—same food, same mismanagement, same hopelessness.

As we walked onto the field, we could hear the crowd mocking us. "It's not about whether Somalia will lose," someone said, "but by how much."

We lost 3–0.

Throughout the tournament, our management never treated us like professional athletes. We were eliminated, and the next day we returned home in silence.

More than anything, we feared getting seriously injured. We knew there would be no medical support, no post-injury care, not even a follow-up call. If you got hurt, you were on your own.

How can any individual—or any team—be expected to perform under those conditions?

When we returned to Mogadishu, the team management handed each of us $200.

No one complained.

We all came from war-torn, poverty-stricken neighborhoods and were simply grateful for whatever we received.

But I hadn't been quiet in Tanzania, and I didn't stay quiet in Somalia either.

That was the beginning—and the end—of my career with the national team. They didn't want someone who spoke up, someone who dared to question the system.

No one from the team stood by me. Some even went to the management to report what I had said, hoping to win favor with the scouts and coaches. If I had kept my head down and followed orders—like the rest—I might still be part of the Ocean Stars.

But I couldn't live that way.

"I would rather kill myself than live the life of an obedient dog. I want to play with dignity," I told my coach.

When I walked away from the national team, I walked away with purpose.

My goal was clear: I wanted to open a football academy in my hometown, Kismayo.

Somalis are naturally gifted footballers.

We play in the Spanish style—quick touches, precision passing, clever movement. It's a technique built on intelligence rather than brute strength: minimal energy, maximum efficiency.

With the right training, proper nourishment, and genuine motivation, Somalia can produce exceptional players—players who can compete with the world, and win.

Have you ever seen birds in cages, who can no longer fly? Same like those caged birds, we too lived in a kind of captivity. We were surrounded by chaos—war, poverty, corruption—yet we carried on.

Image Credits: AI generated image by Malick Mahmood

Aaliyah

Have you ever seen birds in cages, or those with clipped wings—birds who can no longer fly? God gave them wings so they could soar freely in the sky. That was their purpose. That was their right. Yet even behind bars, or grounded by human hands, they continue to sing. They hop from perch to perch, they eat, sleep, even reproduce. They seem content, as if they've accepted a life far less than what they were created for. But I can't help but wonder—Are they truly content? Or have they simply forgotten what it means to fly?

Like birds with clipped wings, we too lived in a kind of captivity. We were surrounded by chaos—war, poverty, corruption—yet we carried on.

We danced at weddings, ate what little we had, found ways to laugh. We made love. We brought children into this broken world. Even in our pain, we tasted moments of pleasure.

That is the strange resilience of the human spirit: to suffer deeply, yet still search for joy—to live half-free, and still dream of flying.

Football was the focus of my life.

And when I think about it, I'm reminded of a girl named Aaliyah. I met her because of football—and she became my first love.

One otherwise ordinary afternoon, I was playing barefoot with friends. We were dusty, loud, and our ball was nothing more than a bundle of socks.

Then, in the middle of that messy joy, I saw her.

She walked past the field in a black dress and a blue *hijab*. Slender, graceful—what stood out most was her purity. She didn't seem to belong to this dusty world we were in.

I quickly stepped aside, pretending to be someone important—a young man, barefoot and proud, trying hard to look casual. It must have looked hilarious. But in that moment, I hoped she'd notice me. She did—but maybe not in the way I had imagined.

That happened just six months before we left Somalia. Aaliyah came into my life like a stray bullet, and I was the collateral damage.

It was truly, deeply, madly—love at first sight.

I asked my friends about her. One of them knew her and told me her name was Aaliyah. "But don't even think about it," he warned. "If you see her dad and brothers, you'll understand. Those men are like lions—they'd tear you apart and eat you alive." We all burst out laughing.

The warning only made her seem more mysterious, more untouchable. And then, as boys do, we kicked the socks ball back into play and let the moment fade into dust and sweat.

The story of Aaliyah is one I've never shared—until now. It's been a secret buried inside me for years.

But I'm sharing it now to show the world that the hearts of Somalian youth bleed not only from bullets and bombs, but also from lost love.

In Somalia, it's hard to marry unless you have a steady job, money, and the means to provide. No father wants to give his daughter to someone who can't promise her a secure life. And I—I was just a barefoot boy with a dusty football and big dreams. Dreams that didn't count for much in a world where survival always came first. Still, I couldn't get Aaliyah out of my head. I had to find a way— any way—to get closer to her.

Eventually, an opportunity came.

She had a younger brother who didn't know how to play football, so I volunteered to coach him.

Who better than someone who had once played for the national team?

It didn't take long to become his friend. Soon we were playing near their house. Whenever we asked him for water, he'd take us to his home. I'd wait outside while he went in, always positioning myself so I could get a glimpse through the doorway. And often, I saw her—just for a few seconds—but it was enough to keep my heart racing for hours.

This quiet ritual continued for a while.

Then one day, she noticed me. And when the moment felt right—safe—I slipped her my cell number.

It wasn't long before she called.

"Yousuf, can you please get me some tablets? I have a headache," she said. It wasn't a request—it was a command. And like a servant obeying his queen, I fulfilled it without hesitation.

It was late at night. The streets weren't safe. I had to walk a long distance to find a pharmacy. But none of that mattered.

When I returned, she came to the front door. Despite the darkness, I could see her smile.

She took the medicine through the half-open door and whispered a soft thank you.

That moment lit up my entire night.

After that, we began talking more often on the phone. She shared her stories, her life, her little heartbreaks. And I poured out my thoughts and dreams.

I felt like we were slowly building something real—fragile, but real.

Eventually, I asked if we could meet in person. "Someday," she said. "I'll let you know when the time is right."

Then one day, out of the blue, she called:

"I'm going to visit my relatives. You can meet me there."

"I know the house," I replied, trying to stay calm. But inside, I was flying. It felt like she had just asked me out on our first date.

I put on my best clothes, my cleanest shoes, and raced to that house—my heart pounding with hope.

I saw her before she saw me.

She was gently scolding some parents for not keeping their children clean—and then helping those same children wash themselves. She had a small towel in one hand and a bucket of water in the other. Her sleeves were rolled up. Her face glowed with sincerity.

To me, she looked like an angel.

Right there, standing quietly at the doorway, I realized something: Aaliyah wasn't just a girl I liked. She was the kind of woman I wanted in my life. The only one who ever made me think—truly think—about marriage.

That day, I made a silent promise to myself: As soon as I earned enough money, I would marry her.

We started meeting more often. On quiet street corners. In her doorway. Any place that offered a sliver of privacy. We didn't talk about love. We talked about the poor. The hungry. The neglected children. She wanted to help them. I wanted to help her help them. She would talk, and I could listen to her for hours.

I was completely smitten.

We never formally expressed our feelings. No confessions. No promises. But I didn't need to hear the words. I was certain she liked me. I could feel it in her presence, her tone, her silence.

One day Aaliyah called me, her voice trembling with frustration. "There's a boy at school who's bothering me," she said.

She hadn't told her brothers. Not her father. She told me. She trusted me.

I didn't hesitate. I went straight to the boy. He was from my neighborhood; someone I knew—someone I didn't want to mess with. But that didn't matter. I was angry. Protective. Maybe even foolishly brave.

When I confronted him, he narrowed his eyes and asked, "What is she to you? What did she tell you?"

His question caught me off guard. I should've spoken to Aaliyah first. I should've known what story she had given him—if any. But I didn't think. I just said, "She's my girlfriend. That's all you need to know. Stay away from her."

I don't know why, but he backed off. Maybe it was the look in my eyes. Or maybe he realized she wasn't alone anymore.

Later, when we met Aaliyah asked, "What did you tell him?" I paused. I wanted to be honest. But I didn't know how she'd feel about me calling her my girlfriend. So I shrugged and said, "I didn't say much. Just made it clear he shouldn't bother you again." She didn't press further. But that moment stayed with me. Not because I was proud of what I did—But because for the first time, she had put her safety in my hands.

About three months before I left Kismayo, Aaliyah called me. Her voice was bright, almost bubbling with excitement.

"Yousuf, I'm getting married!" she said. "To my cousin. You know—he lives abroad. He has a good job, makes a lot of money. I'm so lucky…"

She kept talking—words pouring out like a flood—but I couldn't hear them.

It felt like a bullet had gone through my chest. My mind buzzed. My ears rang. The only thing I could process was that I had just lost her. And the worst part? I'd never truly had her to begin with.

When she finally paused, waiting for me to say something, all I could manage was: "Best wishes." But inside, I was boiling. I was hurt. I was confused.

How could she do this to me?

Didn't she know what she meant to me?

Hadn't she seen it in my eyes, heard it in my voice?

It had never occurred to me I could lose her to someone else—especially not to her cousin.

But reality hit hard:

I couldn't compete with him. He had everything I didn't—money, stability, a future. And I couldn't tell anyone. Not my friends. Not even my mother.

I carried the heartbreak alone.

I stayed upset for two reasons. The first, of course, was that she was getting married. But the second was something deeper—I needed answers from her. I couldn't just walk away without knowing why, so I sent her an email.

I poured my questions into it, each one weighted with the pain of what I was feeling, and then I waited for her response.

I knew she read it. I could feel it. But she never replied.

Then one day, I saw her online on an internet messaging site, and I couldn't hold it in anymore.

I asked her—plain and simple—why she hadn't replied to my email.

It didn't take long for her to respond.

"I never thought of you in that way. You were always like a friend and brother to me," she wrote.

Those words cut through me like a knife. But I knew it wasn't the full truth.

It was the version she needed to say—because her cousin had everything I didn't. Money. Status. A house. A future. And I had nothing.

After that, I never tried to see her or speak to her again. The pain of it all had shattered something inside me, something I didn't think I could fix.

She had no idea that, for her, I had even made a decision that would change the course of my life. I would rejoin the national football team. I would push myself to the limits, to a place where I could stand tall, where I could become someone worthy. And maybe then, I thought, I would have a chance to ask for her hand in marriage.

It became increasingly difficult for me to stay in Kismayo.

The city, with all its reminders of Aaliyah, felt like a weight pressing down on me.

I often found myself asking why it had to be her, why it wasn't one of the other girls who had shown interest in me.

I had turned down many, girls who had genuinely expressed a desire for a relationship, yet it was Aaliyah who had taken up so much of my heart.

I believed it was God's will for me to experience this pain. It was my fate, my destiny.

After about a week, I came to the painful realization that it made no sense to keep stalling my life for someone who hadn't cared about me the way I had cared for her.

I was ready to leave Aaliyah and her story behind, to turn the page.

The two things I had loved most in this world—after my mother—were football and Aaliyah. Both had been taken from me in Somalia.

Football, I knew, would be easier to pursue elsewhere—maybe in Germany.

But whether I would find someone I could care for like I had cared for Aaliyah, I didn't know. That question remains unanswered, even today.

About two weeks before I was set to leave Somalia, I told my friends at the cinema that I had made my decision.

Cinemas in Kismayo weren't like those in the developed world. Ours was a tent where movies were projected onto a small TV screen connected to a DVD player. We sat on rocks, not comfortable chairs.

Image Credits: AI generated image by Malick Mahmood

Cinemas in Kismayo weren't like those in the developed world. Ours was a tent where movies were projected onto a small TV screen connected to a DVD player. We sat on rocks, not comfortable chairs. My friends were fond of watching Indian movies dubbed in our Somali language, but I preferred Hollywood films.

After the show, as we walked out, I shared my decision with them. "I'm leaving Somalia," I told them firmly.

As expected, we argued about the hardships of the journey. But this time, the conversation was brief.

In the end, they all agreed that it was probably the best decision. Razzaq and Saeed decided to stay behind, but Ahmed, as I had hoped, would join me.

By the time we separated, it was late, and I was walking faster than usual.

Ahmed caught up with me. "So when are we leaving?" he asked.

"In two weeks," I replied.

His eyes widened in surprise. "Two weeks is too soon."

"If we have to do it, then let's do it. There's no point in delaying it," I said, stopping to make my point.

Ahmed stood there, listening. It was a pivotal moment of my life, one that marked my resolve.

"So where will the money come from?" Ahmed asked as we began walking again.

"We'll work and save what we can," I explained, and went on to tell him how we could get a free ride out of Somalia. I knew truck drivers in the area who would take us for free in exchange for us helping load the trucks along the way.

"And where exactly are we going?" Ahmed asked, already starting to see me as his guide.

"Germany," I replied. By that time, we had reached the restaurant where we had witnessed the murder of a man and a little girl, I stopped across the street. Ahmed saw where I was looking, and he knew right away what I was thinking. It had been a horrific scene, one that haunted both of us.

"How could we ever forget that small, innocent child bleeding to death right in front of us?" I said.

We both stood in the same spot where we were that day when it had happened, frozen in memory.

"Remember how the rice was flowing out of the man who was shot in his stomach?" Ahmed reminded me, and everything came back in slow motion.

Ahmed and I had been sitting on the footpath across the street from the restaurant. We saw a man leave the restaurant and walk over to the wash basin outside. A little girl, maybe four or five years old, stood beside him. She was the daughter of the restaurant owner, perhaps holding soap or a towel for him. As they stood there, out of nowhere, another man appeared and shot the man in the stomach. The bullet passed through him and struck the little girl in the neck.

The assailant didn't stop there. He continued shooting the man even as he lay dead on the ground. The child was rushed to the hospital in an ambulance, with same broken horn but soon, she bled to death.

That night, when I went to bed, I felt like I was already on the road. I began to dream about my new life, what it would be like to live in a peaceful country.

Even the thought of the journey itself brought me hope. That hope became my strength, pushing me to work harder and save money for the journey ahead.

I knew my parents would never agree to my plan, so I didn't tell them. But there was no doubt in my mind that this journey would be a perilous one, a journey through the valley of death.

"They are caravans of the dead," my mom would say whenever she heard about someone leaving for Europe.

She had no idea that one day her own son, her eldest, would join those caravans of the dead, as she called them.

As the day of departure drew closer, I found myself reflecting on everything I would be leaving behind.

Kismayo was my home, and though I couldn't wait to escape, I knew I would miss my family, my friends, the familiar streets.

The memories of the internet cafes, where I would go to unwind.

But above all, I wondered how I would ever forget Aaliyah—my first love.

My decision to leave Somalia was firm, but the reality of it weighed heavily on me. I spent countless hours lying in bed, staring at the ceiling, tears silently streaming down my face as I thought about my mom. I knew I would miss her more than anything. The thought of dying along the way haunted me, and I could almost hear her wailing in grief. The very idea of causing her that pain was unbearable, yet it was a thought that lingered, robbing me of sleep at night and clouding my mind during the day.

I guess my mom noticed something was off, because she would often ask, "Yousuf, are you alright? You seem like you want to talk about something."

"I'm fine, Mom. It's just Mohammed. I think about him sometimes," I would reply, lying through my teeth.

The truth was, no mother would ever let her child go on such a journey through the valley of death, and I couldn't bring myself to tell her the real reason behind my turmoil.

Before I left Somalia, I made a pledge to myself: once I had enough money, I would return and fulfill my dream.

I envisioned a football academy, one that stood out for its beauty and purpose. The grounds would be immaculate, and the players would have access to the kind of equipment and facilities that rivaled international-level teams. But more than that, they would have self-respect and the will to compete, always pushing until the very end.

I pictured the academy being linked with the local schools, creating a synergy where only those boys who attended school regularly and excelled academically would be allowed to join.

It wasn't just about football; it was about shaping better individuals—athletes with discipline, focus, and a sense of responsibility to their community.

As the day to leave Somalia drew nearer, I found it harder to play football.

My focus had shifted to earning money, preparing for the journey.

It didn't bother me too much, though.

I knew that if I could make it to the other side, I'd have a better chance of pursuing football professionally.

But with that day looming, anxiety began to build inside me. I wanted to share my plans with my parents, to discuss what was about to happen, but I knew it was impossible.

On my last Friday in Kismayo, I brought the ingredients for *ugali*, my favorite dish, to my mom so she could cook it for me.

As I sat down to eat that meal, I couldn't help but think that this might be the last time I would enjoy such a simple yet meaningful moment with my family—my parents, brothers, and sisters.

Ahmed and I had no idea what awaited us on this journey, but we were determined, ready to face the hardships ahead.

We were about to embark on the valley of death together, hoping that it would lead us to a better life.

Meanwhile, Aaliyah married her cousin a few weeks before I left Kismayo.

It was a bittersweet moment.

The one person I had cared for deeply had moved on, while I was left to grapple with my dreams and the pain of unfulfilled love.

Kismayo to Addis Ababa, Ethiopia

"Tomorrow we say goodbye to Kismayo and travel toward the land of our dreams."

"Yes," was all Ahmed could say.

Earlier, we had made arrangements with a truck driver who was leaving around noon the following day.

He had agreed to let us ride for free in exchange for our help loading and unloading cargo along the way to Addis Ababa, Ethiopia.

He told us it would take five to seven days to get there.

"And this is our last evening in Kismayo—the land of our forefathers," Ahmed said, sounding distant and absorbed.

"It is not," I replied. "We shall surely come back once things get better."

Ahmed was behaving strangely, and I couldn't tell if he was lost in thought or just as eager as I was.

I began wondering if he would be able to make it through to the other side. I couldn't help but assess the differences between us—were there any?

Neither of us had any special training. We were about the same build. If long days of football under the hot sun counted for anything, then we were equally prepared.

So I told myself: If I can do it, then he can too.

Migration as refugees was our destiny—and we were not alone.

Even today, thousands are making this journey or preparing for it. Some will get through, and some will not.

Politicians in Somalia and across Africa make meaningless statements whenever there's a tragedy—like when an overcrowded boat capsizes in the Mediterranean and hundreds drown. They say things like, "These youngsters should not make this journey. They must not risk their lives."

But do they ever consider what choices we actually have?

To us, life in Somalia felt like a dead end.

Since that day, two weeks ago when we met outside the cinema, Ahmed and I had started working small jobs to save enough money to reach Libya.

According to our plan, we wouldn't need money beyond that point.

I had read online that smugglers in Libya offered a free ride to anyone who could steer a boat or operate a GPS.

"So what exactly is the plan? And do we have enough money to reach Europe?" Ahmed asked while sipping his tea.

I think it was his third or fourth cup.

I only watched and listened.

I neither smoke nor drink tea or coffee. Sometimes people insisted I have a cup, and in those situations I'd usually wait for it to cool and then gulp it down like water.

"That tea will kill you, Ahmed," I said, pointing at his cup.

"Yes, maybe. But some bullet will probably get to me first," Ahmed snapped back.

We were talking about our journey from Kismayo to Addis Ababa and beyond.

Ahmed didn't speak English, but I was comfortable with it after spending time online.

That made me the researcher, the planner, and—since Ahmed trusted me with it—the keeper of our money.

Ahmed knew that we would first head to Addis Ababa, the capital of Ethiopia, and that this part of the journey would be relatively straightforward. We talked about it every day while working.

"Yes, you're right. It's easier," I agreed, "but we can't ignore the Ethiopian border forces. If they catch us, they'll imprison us in underground holes."

"*Insha'Allah*, we'll be safe," Ahmed replied.

"From Ethiopia, we'll go to Khartoum in Sudan. From there, we'll cross into Libya."

"And then from Libya, we'll go to Europe by boat," Ahmed added.

"Yes, and you'll be steering it while I navigate with the GPS."

"Who'll be the captain—me or you?" Ahmed asked with a grin.

"Of course I'll be the captain. The captain gives the directions," I declared proudly.

"Oh yeah? And what if I don't steer it the way you tell me to?"

We both burst into laughter and kept joking about it. For a moment, it felt like we were just two boys dreaming big. But deep down, we both knew we were heading into the unknown.

Despite our anxiety, we were also excited—we were beginning a journey of hope.

We had always longed to escape the bloodshed, tyranny, and oppression that surrounded us.

We wanted to reach a place where we had the right to live, to breathe, to eat, to be at peace—and eventually, to die in peace.

"Yousuf, are you sure we'll reach Europe in twenty or thirty days?" Ahmed asked casually.

"Damn sure, Ahmed. Don't worry about anything. Just do as I say and I'll get you to Europe," I reassured him as he took his final sip of tea.

But inside, I knew better.

This journey could easily turn into a nightmare. It could get one—or both—of us killed.

"Ahmed, my friend," I asked again, probably for the hundredth time, "do you really want to go? I mean... are you having second thoughts?"

I asked not just out of concern, but because I never wanted to force anyone into something so dangerous.

I knew the risks.

Anything could happen.

Another reason I brought it up that day was Aaliyah. For me, losing her—and everything she did to me—was an immediate reason and a huge part of why I wanted to leave. But Ahmed hadn't experienced anything like that. That difference puzzled me.

"Yousuf," he said firmly, "I've told you again and again—I'm a grown man. I know what I'm doing. I'm making this journey in search of a better life, just like you. I want to provide for my family."

Ahmed was still talking as we stepped out of the restaurant.

As usual, he had grown emotional.

"I trust you," he continued. "You're not some thug trying to lure me into a trap. I've willingly chosen to travel with you to Europe, and I'm grateful you're taking me along."

His words lifted a weight off my shoulders. They relieved me of the guilt I'd carried for encouraging him. And he was right—this journey wasn't about dragging him into danger.

If anything, I was offering him a path forward, a chance at something better.

In truth, I was leading him out of darkness into light— away from the shadows that hung over Kismayo.

We were part of a generation that had grown up watching Somalia drink our blood.

Mohammed, our friend.

The girl in the restaurant. The one shot in the prison cell. The police officer whose blood had spilled into the sink. All of them—victims of bloodthirsty Somalia.

On our last night in Kismayo, neither of us went home to sleep.

Instead, we chose to spend it with friends.

I knew that if I went home, it would be hard to keep my travel plans hidden from my mother. And if she found out, she'd never let me leave Somalia.

We went to Razzaq's house, where Saeed later joined us.

It was May—when the nights are usually cold—and the four of us sat outside, enjoying the soft breeze.

Spending nights out wasn't a big deal for us. All we had to do was inform our parents, just so they knew we were safe.

"So, when are you guys leaving?" Saeed asked, breaking the silence.

"We're still short on money," Ahmed replied casually, dodging the question with practiced ease. "So… we're not sure yet."

None of them knew our real plans, and we wanted to keep it that way.

"But you'll tell us once you know, right?" Razzaq pressed, curiosity in his voice.

"Of course. Why wouldn't we?" Ahmed responded, glancing in my direction.

It was too dark to read his expression, but I knew exactly what was going through his mind.

We had already discussed that once we left, our friends would quickly figure it out.

They'd probably go straight to our parents. But by then, it would be too late to stop us.

Once we were far enough, even our parents would have no choice but to accept it.

We had agreed to call them either during the journey or after reaching Europe.

"Come with us," I said, changing the topic—and trying one last time to convince them. "There's nothing left for you in Kismayo."

Razzaq and Saeed shook their heads.

They said they couldn't afford the journey.

Besides, they were beginning to believe that things in Somalia might finally turn around.

Al-Shabab had been defeated in Kismayo, and they were hopeful the fighting would soon end.

"It won't end," I said firmly. "It's going to get worse. You'll see."

The night slipped away quickly.

Then, as we heard the call to *Fajr* prayer from the mosque, we all stood up and headed off to pray.

Razzaq and Saeed left after Fajr prayers.

They told us a building contractor had hired them, and they needed to reach the construction site early in the morning.

We had always gone to work together, but ever since Ahmed and I had made our final decision to leave Somalia, we had started going separately.

We bid farewell to our friends, telling them we were headed to the market to load a truck.

What we didn't tell them was that we'd be leaving on that truck.

After parting ways, Ahmed and I stopped at a roadside restaurant for breakfast.

As we sat down, we heard the sharp, broken cry of an ambulance horn wailing from far away.

Ahmed and I exchanged a look but said nothing. I didn't run toward the hospital that day.

This time, I was planning to run very far away from it.

"Can we just go now?" Ahmed asked, fidgeting. "Let's load the truck and leave early."

The sound of the siren had rattled him.

"Everything in its time, Ahmed," I said, trying to calm him down.

Just then, I noticed a boy polishing shoes nearby.

"Let's get our shoes done," I said, motioning him over.

We ate breakfast while the boy quietly polished our shoes.

I offered him a cup of tea.

Life had taught me humility, and I've never believed in looking down on anyone.

No one has the right to judge another by their social status.

Survival in Kismayo was hard.

We paid for our meal, gave the boy his money, and left the restaurant.

On the way to the truck, we agreed to make our farewell calls.

We knew we might not get another chance after we boarded.

We stopped at a public call office (PCO).

"Yousuf, this isn't going to be easy," Ahmed said. "But we have to be careful. We can't let them know our plans."

I nodded silently.

My hands trembled as I dialed my mother's number.

It was hard to steady my voice and even harder to hold back my tears.

"Yousuf, are you alright? Where are you?" she asked.

I could tell she heard the difference in my tone.

I took a long breath and tried to sound normal.

"I'm fine, Mama. Just heading to the market to find some work," I said.

That day, I was neither fine nor safe. But I hung up, carrying the weight of my silence with me.

After I called my mother, I felt strangely energized.

I hadn't told her about our plan, yet the way she showered me with prayers, it felt as if—deep down—she knew.

As if she were silently sending me off, blessing my journey without needing to know the destination.

By early noon, we had finished loading the truck.

It was packed with everything from sacks of salt to containers of diesel—supplies for Ethiopia.

Since Ethiopia is a landlocked country, it depends heavily on neighboring ports for trade.

After Eritrea declared independence in 1991, Ethiopia lost Assab, its only seaport, and Somalia had become a critical supply route.

Before we departed, the driver invited us to join him for lunch.

Ahmed was hungry, so he went along.

I didn't. Eating before a long road trip always made me nauseous.

I don't remember the exact date, but I know it was sometime during the month of May 2013 when we left Kismayo.

It was late afternoon when the truck gave a slight jerk and rolled forward, leaving behind the city we had always known.

Ahmed and I sat on top of the cab, silent as we passed streets we'd walked so many times—places filled with memories of childhood and friendship.

My heart grew heavy.

I was leaving behind the soil where I was born, where every corner held a piece of my life.

Neither of us spoke.

We were each lost in thought—thinking about our families, our homes, our past.

I turned in the direction of my house.

I couldn't see it from where we were, but it felt as though nothing stood between us.

In my mind's eye, I could see my mother moving through the house, doing her daily chores as she always did.

Tears blurred my vision as I silently prayed—prayed for her safety, for my father, for my brothers and sisters.

That moment of departure tore something inside me.

Kismayo is a large city, so it took a while to reach its outskirts and finally merge onto the road to Addis Ababa.

"Do you think we made the right decision?"

Ahmed's question pulled me out of my thoughts.

"Yes, I'm sure," I replied, then looked at him. "What about you, Ahmed? You're still with me in this, aren't you?"

"We're already in it," he said, pointing behind us. "Can't you see? Kismayo is gone."

The city had disappeared into the horizon.

Then, as if trying to shake off the heaviness, Ahmed began to recite lines from Hadraawi's *Jacayl Dhiig Malagu Qoray*—Has Love Been Blood-Written.

The setting sun cast a golden glow across the sky.

I joined him, and together we sang:

"*Jacayl dhiig malagu qoray.*
Wali ruux maloo shubay.
Lafta saanta dhabarkiyo,
Ma u dheegay dhabarka?"

(Has love been blood-written?
Has marrow yet been poured for it?
A person peeled the skin from their back or ribs—
Has expression of this been offered in flesh?).

I've always been a fan of Hadraawi—often called the Shakespeare of Africa.

A revolutionary poet, he spent years in prison after the government accused him of fueling civil unrest with his words.

Mohamed Ibrahim Warsame (1943 – 2022) known as Hadraawi, was a Somali poet, philosopher and songwriter. Hadraawi has been likened by some to Shakespeare and his poetry has been translated into various languages.

But to me, he was a truth-teller. His poetry captured the pain, the soul, and the struggle of Africa.

This particular poem, though sung by the legendary Magool as a love song, had deeper roots. Few people know that Jacayl Dhiig Malagu Qoray was inspired by a real story—of a young Somali man who wrote letters in his own blood for Magool.

Night had fallen.

The truck came to a stop in front of a roadside restaurant, and the driver called us down for dinner. This time, I joined them.

I knew we weren't traveling any farther that night.

Before we left Kismayo, the driver had told us he didn't drive after dark.

He would sleep in the cab, and we could sleep on top.

It wasn't my first night away from home—I had traveled before, for the CECAFA tournament—but that night, lying on top of the truck's cab and watching the stars, I missed my mom and my home deeply.

Neither of us could sleep.

I glanced at Ahmed; he, too, was staring at the sky.

We drove out early the next morning.

For the next few days, the truck rolled steadily onward—each kilometer taking us farther from the place we belonged and closer to where we wanted to go.

Along the way, we made stops to load and unload cargo, and to refuel.

The driver knew the route well and seemed to have a fixed plan for where to stop each night.

He didn't share many details with us, and we weren't tourists—we didn't explore the cities we passed through.

We weren't alone on the truck.

It carried other passengers—poor folks traveling from city to city, unable to afford bus fare, so they hitched rides on cargo trucks like this one.

Magool (Halima Khaliif Omar 1948 - 2004), was a Somali singer. Few people know that *Jacayl Dhiig Malagu Qoray* was inspired by a real story—of a young Somali man who wrote letters in his own blood for Magool.

The journey from Kismayo to Addis Ababa had been surprisingly smooth, even uneventful.

"Yousuf," Ahmed said one afternoon as we rested in another unfamiliar town, "there's something I don't understand. When it's this simple to migrate, why don't more people try it—rather than live humiliated in refugee camps? I mean, look at us. We made the decision, and we're doing it."

He spoke like this was some kind of road trip.

"It's fate, my brother," I said, pulling myself up onto the cab again.

"Theirs is to be there. Ours is to be here."

As the truck pulled out of yet another dusty town, our conversation turned toward the men who had taken up arms—those who killed and looted to survive.

"The mind can't tell right from wrong when hunger and death are everywhere," Ahmed argued. "How can a brain think clearly when it's consumed by fear?"

"Are you trying to justify their violence?" I asked, knowing this was not the first time we'd clashed on the subject.

He stayed quiet for a moment, then nodded slightly. "In a way, yes. I'm trying to understand it… maybe justify it, to an extent."

"Why?" I pressed. "How could you do that? Islam doesn't permit it. No religion does."

"I know. But don't you think these moral values only apply to people who are in control of their senses?"

"Ahmed, if you're saying that militants are not in their right minds, I might agree. But if you're trying to say we should sympathize with them, I can't accept that."

Sometimes it was hard to argue with Ahmed. He had a way of blurring the lines.

At our last stopover, the driver mentioned that the next town we would cross marked the Ethiopian border.

But there was no formal checkpoint, no visa office.

It felt like a single town split between two nations—half in Somalia, half in Ethiopia.

"We're in Ethiopia," I told Ahmed.

"So how much farther to Addis Ababa?" he asked, looking around as if Ethiopia would somehow look different.

"According to the driver, we're about halfway there."

"So, another three days?" he guessed quickly.

"Roughly," I replied, but my mind was still stuck on our debate.

"Ahmed," I said, wanting to finish the conversation once and for all. "I need to settle this about those who take up weapons."

But he cut me off.

"Yousuf, I agree. Our religion and ethics don't allow it. And thank God we never went down that road. But I still feel sorry for those who did. Most of them were driven by their circumstances. Not everyone can take the pressure…"

"Peer pressure," I interrupted.

"It's more than that. For many, it was their only response to a hopeless situation."

"I know what you mean," I said, "but I'd like to remind you of what Prophet Muhammad (peace be upon him) said."

Then I quoted from *Sahih Bukhari*:

"Anyone who believes in God and the Last Day should not harm his neighbor. Anyone who believes in God and the Last Day should entertain his guest generously. And anyone who believes in God and the Last Day should say what is good—or keep silent."

After that, Ahmed said nothing.

He often debated passionately, but in the end, my friends usually came around.

We all believed that no matter how others treated us, we should not stoop to their level.

If we answered cruelty with cruelty, what difference would remain between us and them?

There could never be justification for oppression—no matter the excuse.

That night, we stopped at an Ethiopian roadside restaurant.

During dinner—our sixth night on the road—the driver told us we would reach Addis Ababa the next day.

"Do you think we can find another free ride like this one to Khartoum?" Ahmed asked later, once we were back on top of the cab preparing to sleep.

"I really don't know," I said. "But we'll try."

We continued talking late into the night, trying to plan our next move.

I knew the toughest part of our journey still lay ahead—finding someone who could help us cross into Sudan.

Finally, on the morning of the seventh day, we arrived in Addis Ababa.

The first leg of our journey was complete.

The city was alive with activity.

As the truck neared the market, we could see porters struggling under the weight of heavy loads.

Addis Ababa was unlike Kismayo in many ways, yet as we drove through the bustling streets, the people seemed familiar. Their faces were marked by hardship, much like the ones I had seen back home.

Most of the men on the streets appeared impoverished, and it struck me that the people of Ethiopia, too, were bearing the weight of their own struggles. The poverty, the weariness in their eyes—it all seemed too familiar.

Ethiopia, like Somalia, was suffering.

The difference was only in the details.

Addis Ababa to Khartoum, Sudan

It took us about an hour to unload the truck, and then we were free to leave.

While saying goodbye to the driver, I asked, "When will you return to Kismayo?"

He hesitated at first, saying he wasn't sure of his plans. Then, after thinking for a moment, he added that he might head to Mogadishu instead.

"And after Mogadishu, will you return to Kismayo?" I pressed.

He stepped a bit closer and, referring to Ethiopia's landlocked status, explained there was plenty of work transporting goods between Mogadishu and Addis Ababa. He wanted to make a few runs before heading home to Kismayo.

Then he asked why I wanted to know about his schedule.

"Oh, nothing much," I replied casually. "We might need to return in a day or two..."

Ahmed looked at me, clearly confused, but I ignored his stare and kept talking:

"I was just thinking, if you do head back to Kismayo, maybe we could travel with you again. We'd help with the loading and unloading like before."

He considered it for a few seconds, then nodded. "Come see me early tomorrow at the same spot. I liked your work—I'd be happy to have you along. I'll even pay you this time."

That was exactly what I wanted to hear.

We assured him we'd be there and said goodbye.

"Don't be late—we've got a truck to load," he called out behind us.

I turned and waved.

As we walked away, I noticed a middle-aged man across the road, watching us.

He had been riding with us on the truck since the last stopover. His gaze lingered a little too long.

"Yousuf, what was that about?" Ahmed finally asked once we were out of earshot.

I was surprised he hadn't interrupted earlier.

"We're staying in Ethiopia illegally," I said in a low voice. "You can't imagine what'll happen if the authorities catch us."

"But why did you tell the driver—"

I cut him off before he could finish.

"We have to be careful. If anyone—maybe even someone from Ethiopian secret police—questions the driver about us, he'll say we're with him and leaving tomorrow. That way, we stay out of trouble."

I then nodded toward the man across the road.

"He's been watching us. Could be nothing. Could be something."

Ahmed nodded slowly, realization dawning on his face. "It's not as simple as I thought it would be."

"No, it's not. No matter how careful we are, there's always a chance we'll get caught."

I glanced around, lowering my voice further.

"And do you know what happens if we're arrested?"

I didn't wait for a response. "They throw you into caves—holes dug seven or eight feet underground. No toilets, no light. People live, sleep, and defecate in the same space. Disease spreads fast. People rot there. I swear, I'd prefer death to that."

Ahmed's face tightened with alarm.

"So what do we do now?"

"We find a Somali and ask for help. Someone who's been here long enough to know the way."

Just as I said that, a man walked toward us.

I could tell by his features and the way he carried himself—he was Somali.

We greeted him when he reached us.

After a few polite words, I asked, "Do you know anyone who can help us get to Khartoum?"

He glanced around nervously and leaned in.

"It's not safe to talk about that out here."

Without another word, he motioned for us to follow him to a nearby restaurant.

It seemed we had found our man.

After we ordered tea and snacks, the man leaned forward and asked about our journey plans.

He seemed genuinely sympathetic, but I still chose not to disclose too much.

"As I told you earlier, we're looking for a guide to take us to Khartoum," I said simply.

He nodded, smiling with quiet confidence. "Don't worry. I'll help you find someone who can get you to Sudan."

"How soon can we meet them?" I asked without hesitation.

He glanced at Ahmed, who was finishing his tea.

"As soon as your friend here takes his last sip," he said with a grin.

I had only ordered water and some biscuits.

Since the moment we boarded the truck in Kismayo, I'd felt like I was racing against time—like any traveler desperate to reach his destination.

We left the restaurant and followed the man through narrow streets, turning corners as if we were being led through a maze.

Eventually, he stopped in front of a modest house and knocked.

A young man, just a few years older than us, opened the door and welcomed us inside.

The place had the feel of an informal office—bare but functional.

He led us into a small room furnished with a few stools, chairs, and a table at the center.

Moments later, another Somali man entered.

His face was kind, his demeanor warm.

He greeted us with heartfelt hugs, as though we were long-lost relatives.

It didn't take long for them to understand why we were there.

The conversation naturally turned to Somalia—its struggles, the lost hope of the younger generation, and the steady flow of youth seeking a better future elsewhere.

"So, what's your final destination?" the second man finally asked.

Ahmed, trusting them more than I did, answered quickly, "We want to go to Europe—through the shortest and cheapest route."

The cat was out of the bag.

But perhaps it was time.

Sooner or later, we'd have to trust someone. And these men seemed like the right ones.

Ahmed explained our entire journey plan.

They listened attentively, then the conversation once again drifted to Somalia—especially Kismayo.

Hearing the name of my city brought a rush of memories. My home.

My family.

Everything I had left behind.

"So your name is Yousuf, and you are Ahmed."

Snapping out of my thoughts, I was surprised to hear them say our names.

Ahmed must have introduced us while I had been lost in memories of Kismayo.

I reminded myself to stay focused.

He had no idea that the web of lies and shady dealings would begin right here in Addis Ababa.

Just then, the Adhan for Asr echoed through the streets. The room fell silent.

A moment later, the men stood up, preparing to head to the mosque for prayer.

They were beginning to appear quite decent.

As we moved toward the door to go with them, the second Somali man stopped us.

"You can't go to the mosque with us—not looking like this."

He was referring to our appearance.

We were still covered in dust and grime from the truck ride.

He turned toward the hallway and called out a name.

The same young man who had welcomed us earlier came into the room.

"Take these boys to the barber," the man instructed. "Get them a proper haircut and a shower. Then take them to the market and buy them some decent clothes."

The man who had brought us explained, "You'll stand out too much like this. The Ethiopian secret police are everywhere. You need to blend in."

"Go, clean yourselves up," he added, then patted my shoulder.

"We'll talk later and figure out your situation. You're like my own sons. I feel for you. Above all, you are travelers—and our faith commands us to help travelers."

With that, the two men left for the mosque, and we followed the young man into the streets.

The haircut was quick, and thankfully they kept it short—I liked my hair that way.

Then came the shower, and it felt amazing to finally wash away the journey's dust and fatigue.

Most barber shops in Africa have shower facilities, and for a small fee, you can walk out clean and trimmed.

But the young man didn't let us pay.

Later, he also paid for our new clothes and shoes at the market.

When we returned to the house—whatever it was, a home or an office—both Somali men were waiting for us.

"Did you get them ankle-high shoes?" the second one asked.

"Yes," the young man replied, handing him the shoes.

He inspected them carefully and nodded.

"Good. These will be useful for your journey."

"Thank you for your generosity," Ahmed said with a grateful smile.

I smiled too, but said nothing.

Deep down, I knew we would eventually have to pay for all this. But I didn't want to spoil Ahmed's mood. Let him enjoy the kindness while it lasted.

"No need to thank us, Ahmed. We are brothers in Islam. Everything I'm doing to get you to the Sudanese border is for the sake of Allah alone," said the second Somali man, who by now clearly appeared to be their leader.

He did most of the talking and carried himself like a front man.

"Brother! Why only up to the Sudanese border and not all the way to Europe?" Ahmed asked eagerly, completely taken in by their warmth and generosity.

Just then, a lavish spread of food arrived.

The leader waited for the young attendant to leave before replying.

"The Ethiopian guide I've arranged for you is the best and most honest man I know. He'll take you to the Sudanese border and connect you with the right people to get to Khartoum. From there, another group will take you across the desert to the Mediterranean coast in Libya."

"And from Libya, we'll take a boat to Italy," I added, trying to complete the map forming in my mind.

"Exactly, Yousuf. As you probably know, this is the shortest and cheapest route to Europe."

He clapped his hands lightly and motioned us to begin eating.

"Let's enjoy our meal first. We'll talk more later."

After we'd eaten, they served tea. I tried to decline, but the host insisted. As usual, I let it cool down and gulped it in one go.

During tea, the leader began outlining our travel plan again.

It all sounded good on paper—and frankly, we had no better options.

We had to place our trust in them, whether we liked it or not.

"This evening, we'll take you to a house where others like you are waiting. Your Ethiopian guide will meet you there. He'll take you to the Sudanese border for just a small fee."

I wanted to ask more questions, but he reassured us once again. "I know this guide personally. He's reliable and well-connected. You'll be in good hands."

As we heard the Maghreb adhan, the leader called for the young man.

"Take them to the guide," he instructed. "Tell him these boys are our special guests. Make sure he takes good care of them."

The young man nodded as if he'd done this many times before.

Clearly, we were not the first.

We all stepped outside.

After a round of handshakes and goodbyes, Ahmed and I followed the young man.

The other two Somali men, one who had brought us there and other their leader, turned in the opposite direction, heading for the mosque.

We had taken only a few steps when we heard the leader call the young man back.

Ahmed and I stood where we were and waited.

"They are such kind-hearted people," Ahmed said, visibly moved. "They've spent so much money on us. How will we ever repay them?"

I didn't answer.

My eyes were fixed on the three men who appeared to be in the middle of a tense discussion. Then suddenly, as if reaching a consensus, they shook hands and turned to wave at us.

We waved back.

The young man rejoined us.

Without us asking, he said, "They just reminded me again to take good care of you both."

As we walked, we passed many men heading to the mosque for Maghreb prayers.

I asked the young man if we could stop to pray.

"It's better to keep going now," he replied, glancing around. "Most people are busy with prayers. It's safer this way."

We didn't argue. We continued walking.

About thirty minutes later, we arrived at a modest house near the city center.

The young man knocked.

After a few moments, someone opened the door and quickly ushered us inside.

A short, thin man—who looked Ethiopian—greeted us silently and led us into a room at the back.

Inside, we found a group of twelve to fifteen people sitting quietly. One of them was a girl.

The man pointed to the floor. "Sit. I'll be with you soon."

Ahmed and I exchanged a glance and settled into an empty corner.

"What are these people doing here?" Ahmed whispered.

"They're travelers like us," I replied softly, looking around at the tired, nervous faces.

Something told me the real journey was just beginning.

A few minutes later, the door creaked open again.

The young man who had brought us there gestured for both Ahmed and me to come outside. We followed him to a small courtyard where the Ethiopian man—our supposed guide—was waiting.

"The guide has agreed to take you to the Sudanese border for $175 each," the young man informed us.

"I normally charge $200," the guide added, his voice calm but businesslike. "But your reference is well known to me, so I'm giving you a $25 discount each."

"And how much will it cost to get across the desert to the Libyan coast?" I asked, trying to gauge the full price of our journey. I wanted clarity, but deep down I already knew we wouldn't get it.

The guide gave a casual shrug. "When we reach the Sudanese border, I'll introduce you to the right people. They'll take you all the way to Libya—for a small fee. There's nothing to worry about."

Nothing to worry about. Those words always carried more weight than comfort.

We handed him $350—our precious cash.

The guide nodded and told us to go back to the room we had come from.

The young man who had brought us there smiled and gave us a final pat on the back.

"You're in safe hands now," he said. "Insha'Allah, you'll reach your destination."

Ahmed thanked him sincerely.

I just nodded.

As we stepped back into the dim room, I caught a glimpse of the guide quietly slipping some money into the young man's hand. I couldn't see how much—but it was clear it was more than what those Somali men had spent on our shoes and clothes.

Ahmed sat down looking relieved, while I sat with a knot forming in my chest.

The journey ahead was long. And it had only just begun.

It was long past *Isha* when the Ethiopian guide finally returned.

His face was unreadable, his tone businesslike.

"Later tonight, a truck will come to take all of you to another house, outside Addis Ababa," he announced to the group. "We'll stay there for a day or two. From that point, we leave for the Sudanese border."

He paused, then added matter-of-factly,

"We'll have to walk the entire way from that house to the Sudan border."

No one said a word. No protests, no questions. We all knew the next part of the journey would be on foot. Still, someone from the corner finally asked,

"How many days will it take?"

"If you keep up with me," the guide replied, "three to four days. But I've been with groups who moved faster… and others who were much slower."

The room grew still.

The weight of what lay ahead had begun to settle on everyone.

Then came his warning—sharp and deliberate.

"Be very careful," he said. "The Ethiopian secret police are ruthless. If they catch us, you'll be sent to prison. And Ethiopian prisons," he looked around the room, "are not places you want to see."

His eyes met ours one by one.

"If you want to remain safe," he said slowly, "do exactly as I say. No exceptions."

With that, he turned and left the room.

The silence he left behind was heavy—no one said anything for a long while.

The truck arrived after midnight.

We were herded in quickly—no talking, no questions.

It drove fast, maybe thirty or forty minutes, then screeched to a halt in front of a secluded house.

Again, no time wasted—they rushed us out and into the house.

Inside, we found ourselves in a large, dimly lit hall.

The air was thick with silence and body heat.

Dozens of men and women were already there, huddled in clusters or sitting alone, eyes hollow and wary.

Ahmed and I quietly found a spot in a corner and sat on the cold floor.

"Are all these people going to Europe like us?" Ahmed asked, his voice low and heavy. He sounded tired—more emotionally than physically.

"Maybe," I said. "But why do you worry?"

"I'm going to be captain of their ship," he muttered. "So I have the right to know."

I glanced at him.

I couldn't tell if he was being sarcastic or if he was trying to make a joke. Either way, Ahmed was talking more than usual. Back home, I was the one who led the conversations. That night, I just listened.

We didn't sleep at all.

When daylight broke, the space around us became clearer.

It looked like a farmhouse—isolated and built for this very purpose.

Later that evening, more travelers arrived.

The crowd grew.

We stayed in that house for two days.

The routine was simple, predictable. We prayed five times a day, ate breakfast, lunch, and dinner—meals were basic but hot, served on time. That rhythm gave a strange comfort, even if it didn't ease the growing anxiety.

On the second evening, the Ethiopian guide returned, this time with another full truckload of travelers.

I counted in my head—we must have been close to a hundred now.

The truck also unloaded supplies: vegetables, fruits, bottled water and canned food.

That night, during dinner, the guide gathered us in the main hall.

We sat on the floor, shoulder to shoulder, as he stood before us like a commander addressing a battalion.

"We will leave before dawn," he said firmly. "I want everyone out of the danger zone before sunrise."

Then, one by one, we were handed small backpacks. Each pack contained twelve bottles of water, six tins of pineapple, a pack of dry dates, and some biscuits.

"This is your full ration for the entire journey—up to the Sudanese border," the guide declared.

Murmurs broke out in the crowd.

"That's all?" someone whispered.

The guide raised his voice to silence us.

"It is your responsibility to manage your supplies. Eat too fast and suffer later—it's your choice."

Someone else dared to ask,

"Will this be enough for seven days?"

He didn't flinch.

"If it does or doesn't, I really don't care. Just remember—every extra bottle you carry will weigh you down. The desert doesn't care if you're hungry or tired."

We walked in a single file, just as the Ethiopian guide had instructed. The rules were simple: if he stopped, we stopped. If he ducked, we ducked. If he ran—we ran. No questions.

His words settled over us like dust.

Tomorrow, it would begin.

As planned, we left the farmhouse before dawn, the air still heavy with sleep and uncertainty.

We walked in a single file, just as the Ethiopian guide had instructed.

The rules were simple: if he stopped, we stopped.

If he ducked, we ducked.

If he ran—we ran.

No questions.

He wasn't just carrying his share of food and water. Slung across his chest was something far more valuable: a satellite phone.

Before we had left the farmhouse, he had used it to make a call. He spoke briefly, listened intently, then nodded once.

That was our green signal.

Only after that call did we begin the journey.

Ahmed was walking just ahead of me.

He wasn't talking much now.

None of us were.

After nearly six hours of walking across uneven, dry land, we came upon a small village nestled between gentle hills.

It looked almost surreal—like a mirage.

Our guide stopped in front of a modest tea shop where people greeted him like an old friend.

"We'll rest and have breakfast here," he announced. Within minutes, steaming cups of tea were being passed around, and for a short while, there was a strange calm among us.

No one mentioned Europe.

No one mentioned Sudan.

For those two hours, we just sat on the roadside, sipping tea like locals, as if we had always belonged there.

Before we resumed the journey, the guide told us to refill our water bottles.

"You won't find another source for a long while," he warned.

That's when it hit us—many had thrown away their empty bottles earlier in the day to lighten their load. What we thought was just extra plastic had actually been a lifeline.

We learned a harsh lesson that morning: in the desert, every bottle matters.

We walked again for the rest of the day, the sun growing harsher by the hour.

Blisters formed.

Shoulders ached.

Words were few.

Just before evening, the guide raised his hand.

We stopped.

"We'll spend the night here," he said.

And so we dropped to the ground, exhausted.

There was no shelter—just open land and the sky above, which was slowly fading from orange to black.

The silence of that night would stay with me for a long time.

We hadn't seen another soul since leaving that small village, and the landscape around us had turned increasingly rugged. Low hills surrounded us, and the ground beneath our feet was covered in a thick layer of crushed stone—sharp, uneven, and merciless.

Each step felt like walking on shards, and it was especially difficult for the women, who struggled to keep their balance on the loose, splintered surface, especially when going uphill.

Among us was a middle-aged woman who kept falling behind. Her breathing was labored, and she often paused to catch it.

She told us she suffered from some kind of illness—probably asthma, judging by the wheeze in her voice.

The Ethiopian guide lost his patience.

"If you're sick, why did you choose this journey?" he snapped at her, loud and harsh.

A few others muttered that she was slowing us down and suggested leaving her behind.

Ahmed and I exchanged a glance.

We couldn't do that.

Without a word, we each took one of her shoulders and began supporting her as we walked.

Her steps were slow and trembling, but she clung to us, offering whispered prayers and blessings with every painful stride.

When our shoulders began to ache and our pace faltered, two others stepped in to replace us.

From that point on, we all took turns—two at a time—carrying her forward.

That day, I felt her weight long after we stopped walking. As I bent for Maghreb prayer, the dull ache in my shoulders made it hard to raise my hands. But I also felt something else: a quiet kind of pride.

After prayers, Ahmed and I opened a tin of pineapple and shared it between us.

Sharing food and water became our survival strategy.

With limited rations, generosity wasn't just kindness—it was endurance.

That night, we slept on cold, unforgiving stones. Our blanket was the dark sky, and our bed was the earth beneath. The cold bit into our bones, a sharp contrast to the sunburn we'd earned under the brutal heat of the day.

The tightly coordinated—almost militarily efficient smugglers stayed informed about border patrols through updates on their satellite phones, receiving intelligence from their network of informers spread across regions.

We had over 600 kilometers to cover from Addis Ababa to the Sudanese border. To reach it in ten days, we needed to average 60 kilometers a day. It was grueling.

We woke up before dawn and walked until sunset.

The only breaks came when we reached a village—scattered, small places where we could refill our water bottles or have a cup of tea if luck was on our side.

Our Ethiopian guide always walked a few meters ahead of us.

His eyes were sharp, constantly scanning the terrain.

He stayed in contact with someone on the other side via satellite phone. And whenever he got word of Ethiopian security forces nearby, he'd raise a hand—our signal to duck behind rocks, trees, or whatever cover we could find.

We carried that woman with asthma the entire way.

She became a symbol—of struggle, of compassion, and of the quiet strength that forms when people, even strangers, decide not to leave each other behind.

By the eighth day, desperation had settled over us like the dust in our clothes.

Many among us had exhausted their food and water.

For the past two days, we hadn't passed a single village—no shops, no wells, not even a hint of human life. The sun scorched from above, merciless and indifferent.

Our throats were dry, lips cracked, and eyes hollow.

The woman with asthma finally gave up.

She hadn't had a sip of water since morning, and her strength had vanished.

"Please... put me down," she said in a voice barely louder than the wind.

Her breathing was shallow, her face pale with exhaustion.

I was weak too—my own limbs trembling from thirst—but I went to the guide. He was up ahead, urging us to keep moving, focused and unbothered.

I knew he had water. I'd seen him ration it smartly: just a sip or two at a time, while others among us—less disciplined—had splashed it on their faces or drunk it all in one go.

"I need some water," I said. "She's not going to make it."

"It's my share," he replied coldly, without looking at me. "I'm saving it for myself."

But the others had started to gather around. They saw our exchange and sensed what was happening.

We didn't threaten him—not openly—but the tension was sharp, and he could read our eyes.

We were no longer pleading. Reluctantly, he handed me the bottle. I rushed to the woman and let her drink first. She clutched the bottle with trembling hands, sipped, then drank deeper. She closed her eyes as if the water had brought her back from the edge of death.

When she was done, I put the bottle to my mouth and began gulping.

That first swallow was like liquid life.

But before I could drink more, the guide yelled from behind, "It was only for her!" He sprinted over, snatched the bottle from my hands, and looked at me with fury.

"Do you want us all to die?"

Others, those who had helped carry the woman, now stepped forward too.

"We're all dying," one of them said. "And we all helped her. Why can't we drink?"

The argument turned into a kind of desert conference.

There, under the baking sun, the group demanded fairness.

We collected whatever water bottles were left among us and divided what little was left equally.

"How far is it now?" someone asked, voice hoarse and brittle.

"At your speed?" the guide replied dryly. "Two more days, maybe."

"Can't we get a vehicle to take us to the border?" the woman asked. Her voice had regained some strength, and her words sparked a murmur of agreement.

The guide pulled out his satellite phone and made a few calls. After some time, he returned. "There's a driver," he said. "He's willing to come, but he wants $25 per person."

Without hesitation, everyone agreed. It was a price worth paying. The guide made us hide behind a hill.

"The car can only take twenty people at a time," he explained. "You'll go in groups. The trip will take six hours—three hours to the border, three back."

"What happens once we're at the border?" someone asked.

"There'll be people waiting. They'll take you to Khartoum and beyond," he assured us.

We waited through the afternoon heat, swatting at flies, lying on the hot stones, praying silently.

After Asr prayer, we saw the vehicle approaching.

It was not what we had expected.

From afar, we could see it was just a regular sedan—a yellow taxicab, battered and dusty.

Ahmed stared in disbelief. "Twenty people? In that?"

"I really don't know, Ahmed," I said.

The taxicab screeched to a halt in front of us, the tires kicking up dust as the guide exchanged a few words with the driver through the open window. Then, turning to us, he announced, "All who want to take the first trip, get in now."

People scrambled toward the car in a flurry of motion, but when they reached it, they realized the harsh truth—there was no way more than eight people could fit comfortably inside.

The guide added, "Fare's $500 per trip, so if there are fewer than twenty, your share will increase."

The new arrangement hit hard.

Dividing the fare among just eight people meant an unbearable cost, but there was no choice.

The driver, growing impatient, climbed out of the cab, and without saying another word, began stuffing us into the car.

He made the men lie down on the rear seat, cramming them one on top of the other. Somehow, he managed to fit five passengers into the front seat. We were all squeezed inside, twenty people in total, not counting the driver.

Ahmed and I were among the twenty selected for the first trip. We didn't speak much, just exchanged tired glances as the car's cramped interior became our temporary prison.

The driver turned the engine on, only to immediately switch it off and leap out of the car.

In a heartbeat, he was sprinting away from us.

I heard the guide shout, "Border police, everyone—run and hide!"

Panic set in, and we fumbled to get out of the car.

As I stumbled out, I caught sight of a convoy of military vehicles in the distance, barreling down the road toward us.

The guide's warning had been true.

We scrambled, diving for cover wherever we could, hearts racing as the military convoy passed us by, not stopping, not even noticing.

We waited, breathless, as the dust from the convoy settled. When it was clear, we emerged from our hiding spots, only to see the cab speeding away in the distance.

The driver had stolen our money, fleeing with our fares without a care.

Anger and disbelief surged through the group. "He took our money," someone muttered.

"We've been played." Ahmed and I, along with the others, approached the guide.

"What now?" I demanded. "The driver took our money and ran."

The guide shrugged, his face hardening. "It was your choice to take the ride. Not mine."

Frustration boiled over, but there was nothing we could do. The cab was gone, and walking was now our only option.

"Get moving," the guide barked. "We've wasted enough time already. We're walking until late tonight."

The weight of his words settled heavily upon us. We had already been moving slowly, and now, with our resources drained and the sun beginning to set, the trek felt impossible.

As the sun dipped lower, we reached a small village—a last stop before the Sudanese border.

The guide told us to fill our water bottles, as this was the last chance to do so. Everyone was grateful for the respite, but there was little time.

We moved on again, walking into the night, exhaustion gnawing at us.

By the next day, we were nearing a hill that the guide said would give us our first view of the Sudanese border. Many of us, including Ahmed and me, climbed the hill together, our steps slow and heavy from the relentless journey. When we reached the top, a few figures and vehicles appeared in the distance—Sudan, just beyond our grasp.

"There they are," the guide said, gesturing toward the people below. "Those are the ones who'll take you into Sudan."

"Will they take us to Khartoum?" Ahmed asked, his voice filled with hope.

The guide hesitated. "Depends on who you hire."

I couldn't stand it anymore. "Do we need to find our own way, or are you going to help us like you promised?" I cut him off, my frustration evident.

The guide's face darkened. "I never promised anything. I'm here to bring you to this point. The rest is up to you."

The truth hit hard. We were on our own now, abandoned at the last stretch.

"All of them are the right people," the guide added coldly. "If you want to get to Sudan, you need to move fast. The people down there will leave soon."

Without another word, he turned and started walking back the way we came.

His pace was swift, determined.

I watched him until he disappeared behind a small hill, wondering if he would make it back to Addis Ababa by morning.

Ahmed and many others stared after him, disbelief still lingering in the air. "Is he really going back alone?" Ahmed asked quietly.

"He'll catch a ride from one of the nearby villages," someone muttered.

The rest of us stood there, the weight of the situation pressing down on our shoulders.

Many had already started walking toward the border.

We had no choice but to follow.

"How far is Khartoum from here?" Ahmed asked as we joined the others.

"About 450 kilometers," I said, knowing the distance from my own research. "It's still a long way."

We were on the verge of crossing our second international border, and the journey had only just begun.

The situation unfolded with the men at the border, seeing us approach, jumped into their vehicles and drove straight toward us before we could reach them.

The trucks were older, but sturdy.

Ahmed and I climbed into the back of one that had bench seats crammed with people. It smelled of dust and sweat, the air heavy with the weight of unspoken fears.

The driver, a man with a face hardened by years of survival, agreed to take us to Khartoum for $50 each. He also promised to introduce us to the people who could help us get to Libya.

Ahmed, with a mixture of hope and frustration, told him, "The guide who brought us here promised to help us find the right people."

The driver's eyes hardened as he glanced over at us. "They are Ethiopians. We are Sudanese," he replied coldly, a subtle but clear division in his words.

Ahmed turned to me, seeking my opinion, but I didn't have an answer. I could only shrug, the reality of our situation settling deeper in my chest.

The truck, loaded with passengers, finally pulled away into the night. For the next nine or ten hours, the truck rumbled over the rough roads, the dim light of the headlights barely cutting through the dark.

In the early hours, as we entered the city, someone in the truck whispered that we had finally arrived in Khartoum.

The sound of the Fajr Adhan echoed through the streets, a reminder of the passage of time and the weariness we all carried.

The truck drove through the city, weaving through narrow streets until it stopped in front of a house.

The two men who had been waiting outside rushed forward, practically throwing us into the house. They showed us to the bathrooms, ushering us to freshen up before they promised to serve food.

The air was thick with fatigue as we queued up for showers. Some, too exhausted to care about anything else, collapsed onto the mats spread out on the floor. The truck that had brought us there remained parked outside, and I couldn't help but notice the driver speaking to one of the men who had greeted us.

The two exchanged words, and then, with a quick motion, the man handed something to the driver. I saw the driver slip it into his pocket. They embraced like old friends before the driver climbed into his truck and drove off.

A gnawing suspicion took root in my mind.

The man had given the driver money—why?

Had the driver sold us to these people? I kept the thought to myself, not wanting to stir up unnecessary panic, but the feeling of being commodified, of being treated as cargo rather than people, weighed heavily on me.

The man who had spoken to the driver came back inside, his face unbothered by any concerns. He gathered us in the room and, with a formal tone, said, "From now on, you are our guests. We will help you get to Libya."

"How much will it cost us?" someone asked, the question hanging in the air like a lifeline.

"$300 per person," the man answered without hesitation. There was a murmur of relief—$300 seemed reasonable after the endless uncertainty, the cost of the journey up to this point.

The man left after giving us the details.

Later, two more men entered, one carrying a large pot of food, the other with bread and plates. The smell of fresh food filled the room, and many of us couldn't resist the temptation to eat before succumbing to sleep. But I needed a shower. It had been days since we had a proper one, the last being in Addis Ababa, and my body ached from the grime and exhaustion.

The water felt like a blessing, each drop a moment of relief. When I emerged, refreshed but still weary, I lay down on the floor of the room. I couldn't help but think about how far we had come and what lay ahead. We were being smuggled—moved across borders like illegal goods, our futures dictated by men who made their living from human misery. These were the traffickers, the smugglers, who sold us the illusion of safety in exchange for our desperation.

As I closed my eyes and drifted off to sleep, my mind lingered on the twisted path we had taken, from the edge of one border to the threshold of another. But with the hope of reaching Europe still alive in me, I surrendered to the darkness, not knowing what the next day would bring.

Khartoum to Middle of Nowhere

The loud clang of a spoon against a pot jolted me from sleep, followed by a cheery voice announcing, "Lunch! Lunch!"

It took me a moment to gather myself.

I had slept deeply, maybe for the first time since we'd left Addis Ababa.

The air smelled of freshly cooked food, and I could see others already eating, steam rising from their plates like a temporary comfort in our uncertain world.

Ahmed, fully awake and alert, looked at me and said, "Yousuf, come. We'll have our lunch. You can eat too because we're not going anywhere today." He pointed toward the man dishing out food.

"That guy told me we'll leave tomorrow."

Ahmed had naturally taken charge of our two-man team, and I saw no reason to change that.

Besides, it wasn't like we had any control over the decisions being made around us. The smugglers dictated everything—what we ate, where we slept, when we moved. Our agency had been stripped the moment we paid that first fare in Ethiopia.

We were passengers in someone else's plan, not travelers in our own.

Still, Ahmed's remark about hot food made sense. "When they're courteous enough to serve us hot food," he said, "we must be well-mannered enough to eat it while it's warm."

He said it lightheartedly, but we both knew this hospitality was part of a much darker machine.

As we ate, one of the men announced that anyone who wanted a haircut or needed to buy clothes could come with him.

"We'll leave for Libya tomorrow night," he added, explaining that the delay was due to a security issue.

That word—"security"—had become code for danger. It meant border patrols, checkpoints, or perhaps rival smuggling operations.

The smugglers stayed informed through constant updates on their satellite phones, receiving intelligence from their network of informers and partners spread across regions.

It struck me again how tightly coordinated this underworld was—almost militarily efficient.

Later in the afternoon, the quiet hum of the house stirred again when a new group arrived.

Three girls and two boys.

One of the boys greeted everyone in Somali.

Ahmed immediately sprang to his feet at the sight of the girls, especially one with fair skin and soft features.

I found out later her name was Ayesha—and she reminded me of Aaliyah.

That evening, Ahmed introduced me to the group.

I barely managed to remember names except for a few: Ayesha, and a boy named Hafiz, who had memorized the Qur'an.

The second boy stood out for a different reason.

He was here for love.

"I am here for my girl," he told us with pride.

He intended to get her to Tripoli, and then return home. We didn't know his name, but we called him Lover Boy.

As for his girlfriend, she seemed to look down on everyone.

Even him.

Always giving orders, walking around like she owned the place.

She quickly became Arrogant Girl.

The third girl, soft-spoken and observant, kept mostly to herself—Quiet Girl, we called her.

As Maghreb approached, the Adhan echoed through the dusty streets outside.

Most of us, offered our prayers together.

It was a brief moment of unity and peace in an otherwise unpredictable journey.

But the smugglers, I noticed, did not join us.

They moved about their business, uninterested in the call to prayer—too immersed, perhaps, in the business of borders and bodies.

We had dinner after Isha, a simple meal, but hearty enough to silence the day's hunger.

Afterward, those who smoked or chewed miraa wandered outside to the small garden under the night sky. The house emptied out a bit, voices faded, and the air inside turned still.

I stayed in.

That's when I noticed Ayesha, sitting alone, her back against the wall, her eyes half-closed in thought and a gentle smile playing on her lips—like she had found a moment of peace, or perhaps a memory worth keeping.

I didn't want to disturb her, so I just watched quietly from where I was, caught in the quiet lull of the evening.

Then, out of nowhere, the thought struck me again:

Why do girls have to make this journey?

My mind drifted to a conversation I'd had with a woman earlier on our journey—the one with asthma.

Her story had stayed with me.

She told me she'd been married off at nineteen to an older Somali man visiting from Germany. Her father saw a chance for her to live abroad, for the family to rise in status.

"My father saw only his money and didn't care about my feelings," she'd said.

That man stayed with her for three months, using her like property.

Then he left, promising to send for her soon.

What arrived instead were divorce papers.

She remarried, this time to a local boy who had loved her since they were kids.

Life was hard—they had barely enough to eat. Eventually, he joined a militant group to make ends meet. A year before our journey, he left for Europe, promising to bring her along once he settled.

Then one day, a letter came.

He was with someone else now.

He wanted her to move on.

Another divorce.

"How could anyone just use me and then throw me away like I was some kind of trash?" she asked me that day. There was no bitterness in her voice—just a tired determination.

"If I'm able to get to Germany, I'm going to make everyone recognize me as a human and not trash. I'll prove I can do lots of things and live on my own."

That strength—coming from someone who'd been wronged so deeply—humbled me.

Lying there on the floor, with the faint scent of food still in the air and the murmur of distant conversations fading, I thought about her, and Ayesha, and so many other women who had taken this same dangerous path. Not for dreams of luxury, but for dignity, for survival, for proof that they mattered.

With those thoughts swirling in my head, I eventually drifted off to sleep.

That morning unfolded in the same rhythm we had gotten used to—Adhan for Fajr, brief peace in prayer, and then a few more hours of much-needed sleep. But the real wake-up call came, as always, with the clanging of metal—a pot struck by a spoon.

It was their odd way of announcing breakfast, and despite how annoying it was, we couldn't help but smile at the strange consistency of it.

After breakfast, one of the smugglers entered.

His tone was more serious than usual.

He gathered us and laid out the plan: we would leave after sunset for another location outside Khartoum.

"The real journey will begin tonight from that house," he said, his voice firm.

Hafiz, always direct, asked what everyone was thinking.

"You mean the journey to Tripoli?"

"Yes, tonight we take you to Libya," came the reply.

Then, as expected, came the price: $300 per person—for the fare and the supplies we'd need to survive the brutal crossing.

No one protested.

By now, we were too deep into this journey. Resistance had worn thin. There were no better options, no alternate routes. We had given up comfort long ago—now, we were just trying to preserve what was left of hope.

I didn't speak. Like the others, I simply nodded.

The next leg of our journey—across some of the harshest terrain on Earth—was about to begin.

The journey had resumed, but this time it felt more like an operation than an escape.

The smugglers' instructions were clear and coordinated—travel in groups of five or six, by regular buses to avoid attention, and then get off at the last stop.

When it was our turn, Ahmed and I joined the last group, which included the three girls and two boys who had arrived earlier.

As promised, before departure, each of us received a bag. Mine was heavier than I expected.

Inside were tins of food, a couple of basic clothes, and two water bottles.

The smuggler's warning echoed in my ears: "Hold onto the water bottles even after they're empty. You'll get water only once every twenty-four hours."

That remark hit hard.

It was a reminder of what lay ahead—an environment where water was not just scarce but sacred.

By the time we boarded the bus, it was nearly Isha.

The bus ride was quiet, everyone holding tightly to their bags as if clinging to the last bit of control we had.

After an hour, the bus stopped.

A four-by-four jeep waited for us, its headlights cutting through the darkness.

Without a word, we climbed in.

The vehicle accelerated at terrifying speed, off-road, kicking up dust as we crossed uneven, barren land.

Finally, we reached a cluster of trees around a crumbling building.

The driver gestured for us to enter.

A dim bulb cast long shadows on cracked walls.

Inside, I saw familiar faces—those who had left before us. But there were new faces too—some solemn, some hopeful, some already resigned.

Despite the exhaustion, my heart found a kind of peace when I saw a small corner where I could pray.

I spread my jacket on the dusty floor and began my Isha prayer.

A few others joined in.

When I finished and turned my head, I saw Ayesha in prayer. Her face was calm, luminous in the faint light—a rare moment of serenity in a world that had forgotten what peace felt like.

"Yousuf, you're so black you fade away in the darkness!" Ahmed appeared out of nowhere with his usual mischief.

Even though Ayesha was still praying, I saw a faint smile curl on her lips.

I couldn't hold back my laughter either.

"Yeah, and thank God you arrived," I shot back. "Now everything is glowing bright around us!"

That cracked everyone up.

The whole room echoed with laughter, cutting through the weight of uncertainty that had been hanging over us for days.

After prayers, our group gathered for a lighthearted chat. For the first time in a long while, we felt... normal. The journey so far had gone smoother than expected, and optimism was spreading.

We began estimating our arrival in Europe—maybe two weeks, if all went well.

But then, just after midnight, two more jeeps arrived. The smugglers called us to action.

"Load them up," one of them instructed. "These will take you closer to Libya."

The excitement was electric.

Everyone jumped up and started helping. We loaded the jeeps with cans of petrol and water—our lifelines in the desert—and climbed aboard, fifteen people per jeep.

Soon, we rolled out into the cold, dark vastness of the desert.

I was sitting on the last seat of our jeep, and Ahmed was in front of me on the opposite side.

We wore sock masks—part of the supplies given to us earlier—probably to shield our faces from sand.

The sky above was breathtaking. A blanket of stars stretched endlessly across the heavens, shimmering like silver needles scattered across black silk.

In the middle of the barren land, it felt like we were sailing through the universe.

The driver, unfazed by the shifting dunes and lack of tracks, was talking loudly on his satellite phone, then laughing.

The jeep surged forward faster.

"How do they find their way with no road, no tracks?" Hafiz shouted to me over the roaring engine.

"If they have satellite phones, maybe they have GPS too," I shouted back.

But deep down, I wasn't sure.

The Ethiopian guide who brought us to the Sudanese border had been eerily accurate in his navigation, yet never used any device. I truly believe he used the stars—just like ancient desert nomads.

After a couple of hours, the jeeps came to a halt.

We were told to rest for a while.

The people from the second jeep had already disembarked and were stretching their limbs.

I did the same.

The air was freezing, the silence profound.

We had stopped in a narrow pass between two Rocky Mountains.

The sun had already begun to rise meaning time for Fajr prayer had passed, so I quietly performed *Qada* Fajr.

My connection to God had become my compass—a source of hope, strength, and sanity.

In this sea of smuggling, hunger, uncertainty, and fear, prayer gave me something nothing else could: Peace.

The pain I carried couldn't be explained to someone who hadn't lived it. To understand it, you'd have to leave behind everyone you love, everything you know, and face death every day with no guarantee of tomorrow.

When I finished my prayers, I noticed another jeep approaching us.

It rolled to a stop, and the drivers greeted one another like old colleagues.

There were two men in the new vehicle—clearly part of the same smuggling network.

Not long after, they told us to unload everything from the two jeeps we had come in and transfer it to the newly arrived one.

The new jeep was bigger, but even then, it was hard to imagine how fifteen people from each of the two jeeps, along with all the supplies, would possibly fit onto this single vehicle.

"How do you think we're all going to fit in?" Ahmed whispered to me.

"I guess we'll have to squeeze," I replied, loud enough for others to hear.

A few chuckles followed, but the tension remained.

"This is for your own good," said our driver as he began loosening the rope that held the baggage in place.

"From this point on, it's too dangerous to travel in two jeeps. If the security forces catch you... they'll bury you alive." His words hit hard.

The idea that being captured meant being buried alive left a cold weight in our chests.

No one dared question him after that.

It took us nearly three hours under the punishing sun to unload the supplies from both jeeps and reload them onto the third one.

The new jeep was a flatbed truck, with supplies packed tightly just behind the cabin and piled high in the center.

The women were seated in the narrow spaces between the luggage.

As for the men, we had to sit along the outer edges, our legs dangling down from the sides of the platform.

There was no room to move.

No comfort.

Just tight, raw survival.

By noon, we were back on the move, charging into the wild like a battered caravan of ghosts.

The second driver kept getting instructions via satellite phone, relaying directions to the man behind the wheel.

The jeep tore through the unforgiving desert, bouncing and jolting over rocks and dips.

Every bump slammed our bodies around like rag dolls.

Those of us hanging on the edge—legs exposed and swinging—let out involuntary groans with each jolt. "AHH!" someone would yelp, then fall silent again.

The pain in my legs became unbearable.

They flayed uncontrollably, lost all feeling, and finally went numb.

But no one complained.

Not once.

We all knew this was just the beginning of the real journey. And if we couldn't endure this, we had no business hoping for Europe.

We drove until evening, bouncing through the desert like cargo, not people.

When we finally stopped, the driver told us to get some rest and have dinner.

At first, I couldn't even stand straight—my legs refused to support me.

It took several painful minutes for the blood to start circulating again.

There was no food given to us.

We were told to eat whatever rations had been provided earlier in the bag.

After eating in silence, we lay down on the cold sand and fell asleep under the open sky.

It felt like only moments had passed when the jeep's engine roared to life, followed by the driver blasting the horn repeatedly.

We jolted awake and scrambled to our places like soldiers under fire.

In no time, we were back in the jeep, returning to our "regular seats."

It was nearly midnight when we set off again.

The drivers had switched seats—the original driver was now talking loudly on the satellite phone while the other man drove.

The two of them sat comfortably in the cabin, but they had no idea what we at the back were enduring.

We sat with only our bums on the wooden flatbed, our legs dangling in the air, throbbing with pain and numbness. A thin iron bar bordered the jeep, and we clung to it like our lives depended on it—because they did.

After less than two hours of driving, the second driver suddenly told the first to switch off the headlights and slow down.

The jeep crawled forward in complete darkness for about an hour.

Then, far off to our left, we saw three lights approaching.

"Security people!" the second driver shouted. The jeep banked hard to the right.

Panic washed over us like a sandstorm.

But soon it became clear the approaching vehicles were going in a different direction.

The gap between us widened.

We had dodged a near disaster.

For another hour, we continued driving without headlights, hoping not to encounter anyone else.

When we were finally in the clear, the headlights came back on, and we pushed forward—nonstop—for three or four more hours.

Just after sunrise, the jeep screeched to a stop, and the engine went silent.

I tried to get off but immediately collapsed face-first into the sand.

My legs were dead.

No strength.

No sensation.

I rolled to one side and just lay there, breathing heavily, waiting for my body to return to me.

After a while, I slowly stood up, taking small, shaky steps toward Ahmed, who was also struggling to regain his footing.

We didn't speak at first. Just walked around in silence.

"Although walking from Addis Ababa was tough, this is more painful than that," Ahmed finally said.

"Ahmed, my brother," I replied, "this journey will only get harder. We must stay focused. I believe we can do it."

Eventually, Hafiz and the others joined us, all the men in visible pain.

The women, having sat between the bags, hadn't had to dangle their legs over the edge and were slightly better off.

"How are you, Yousuf?" Ayesha asked gently.

"I'm fine," I said, keeping it short.

We gathered to have breakfast: biscuits and dried dates—meager rations that left us more parched than full.

By the time we finished, nearly all of our drinking water was gone.

Hafiz, Lover Boy, and a few others went to talk to the drivers about the water.

When they returned, they told us that we'd only get more at the next stop.

"How can they do this to us?" Arrogant Girl snapped. "You should've told them we need water now."

But there was no time for protest.

We heard the engine start, and like trained prisoners, we got up and walked toward the jeep again.

As we drove off, I held the iron bar tightly.

My legs screamed in agony with every bump, but there was no relief in sight.

We drove all day without a single stop.

There was nothing but sand, stretching endlessly in every direction.

The sun scorched our skin, our lips cracked, and our throats burned for water.

But the driver didn't stop.

Not even once.

We were deep in the heart of the Sahara now.

And the desert was beginning to show us who was in charge.

"Stop! Stop the jeep!" everyone shouted at once as a man suddenly fell off the back.

The driver hit the brakes and the jeep screeched to a halt.

We all jumped off to check on him.

Luckily, he had rolled into soft sand and wasn't injured. But as soon as he got up, he charged toward Arrogant Girl and slapped her across the face.

It all happened so fast.

Apparently, she had been sitting in the middle, tried to stretch her legs, and kicked him off the edge of the jeep.

Before I could step in, Lover Boy and Hafiz were already on the man—throwing punches, yelling, and wrestling him to the ground.

"Yousuf, stay out of this!" Lover Boy shouted when I tried to intervene.

"How dare he hit my girl?"

By then, Ahmed had rushed to stand beside me.

I stepped between them and held out my hands.

"Look," I said firmly. "It's two against one now. You've already hit him—he's been punished. Let's stop this before it gets worse."

I turned to Lover Boy and Hafiz and explained what had happened—how Arrogant Girl had stretched her legs and kicked him off the jeep.

Slowly, the tension dropped.

Breathing heavily, both sides stepped back.

I urged them to apologize and shake hands. And they did.

Just then, the driver's voice rang out from behind us.

"Yallah! Yallah!" he shouted impatiently.

We hurried back to the jeep.

Someone asked the driver when we'd finally get water.

But instead of answering, he tapped his watch and barked, "Yallah! Security police!"

That was the end of the discussion.

He climbed into his seat, started the engine, and we were off again. We drove non-stop until sunset, the sky slowly turning red behind the distant dunes.

Eventually, we stopped in a rocky, hilly area. The drivers got out and announced we'd rest there for the night.

One of the drivers finally pulled out a large water canister from the luggage and allowed everyone to refill their empty bottles.

Our legs were still in pain—it was difficult even to stand in line. I kept reminding myself, "This journey is tough… but it will eventually end."

When I reached the can, I refilled both my bottles and slowly walked back to Ahmed.

"I guess we're somewhere near the Libyan border now," I said. Ahmed looked at me, surprised. "How do you know that?"

"We've been driving for about 22 hours total, right? If we averaged 70 kilometers per hour, we've already covered around 1,500 to 1,600 kilometers. If they're following the right route, then we're only 300 or 400 kilometers away."

I saw him nod slowly, absorbing the numbers.

After Maghreb, we gathered as a group and shared food again—whatever little we had left.

The man who had fallen off the jeep earlier came and sat with us. "I'm really sorry," he said again. "I shouldn't have hit her."

Ahmed replied calmly, "It wasn't entirely your fault. She did push you, even if it was unintentional."

Arrogant Girl was sitting close by, listening. "I never meant to hit him," she said. "I just stretched my legs a little… it was an accident."

The man sighed. "You do realize," he said, "we're all barely sitting on that jeep. Just our small butts are on the edge, the rest of us is hanging off. Any imbalance, and someone goes flying."

Without missing a beat, Arrogant Girl shot back,

"Your butt is not small."

There was a pause—and then we all burst out laughing, even the man she had knocked off the jeep.

After Isha, we lay down on the cold sand. That night was especially freezing, and we all moved in close for warmth.

I had Ayesha on one side, Ahmed on the other.

Later that night, I felt Ayesha shaking me gently. "Yousuf…" she whispered. "I need to go to the bathroom." Still half-asleep, I grumbled,

"Bathrooms are all around us—can't you see?"

Then I realized others were sleeping nearby, so I lowered my voice. Ayesha was already on her feet.

We walked a short distance away from the group.

I pointed to the dunes and said, "You can go here. Just… be quick."

She stepped away in silence, relieved herself, then returned.

On what must have been the 4th or 5th day, we entered a rocky, mountainous area. In the distance, we spotted a few jeeps and men standing around them. A few passengers noticed too and began shouting "Tripoli! Tripoli!"

"Thanks," was all she said before lying back down.

We curled back up and went to sleep.

At Fajr, we prayed together, and soon the drivers started loading the jeep again.

We left the hilly terrain just before sunrise.

For the next two days, the routine remained unchanged.

We would drive all day, from sunrise to sunset, without stopping. In the evenings, they would let us refill our water, and every morning before departure, they would refuel the jeep.

It was mechanical now.

Endless sand, blistering heat, numb limbs, dry mouths, and the deepening exhaustion of bodies slowly falling apart but still moving forward.

We had travelled hundreds of kilometers by now, and I was sure—we were already inside Libya.

The days had blurred into each other.

Time had no shape anymore.

It felt like we had left Kismayo ages ago.

I hadn't spoken to my mother in days. I kept telling myself I'd call her when we finally reached Tripoli.

On what must have been the fourth or fifth day, we entered a rocky, mountainous area. In the distance, we spotted a few jeeps parked on the slope and men standing around them. A few passengers noticed too and began shouting with excitement, pointing toward the men:

"Tripoli! Tripoli!"

Ahmed leaned over to me.

"Yousuf, have we really made it to Tripoli?"

I looked out carefully.

"There's no way this was Tripoli," I told him. "But this might be the Libyan border."

As we moved closer, I noticed the men were armed—some holding AK-47s, others casually waving them in the air.

Our jeep stopped on a narrow, hilly road leading toward the armed group.

Even before the drivers stepped out, many of the passengers had already jumped off, eager or maybe nervous.

I was still lying on the ground, my legs numb and lifeless from the long ride.

I tried to get up but couldn't.

Just then, a vehicle approached and stopped near us. Three men stepped out.

Our jeep drivers walked over and greeted them in Arabic. Two of the new men were also holding AK-47s.

The third, taller and clean-shaven, seemed like their leader.

This was the first time on our journey that we had seen heavily armed human smugglers.

I finally managed to stand, wobbling as blood rushed back into my legs.

We all gathered around our jeep, watching the interaction.

After a short conversation, the tall leader gave us a quick glance, as if counting us silently, and then the three of them walked uphill, leaving us behind.

Just then, I heard Hafiz call the Adhan for Asr.

We prayed together, right there on the roadside under the open sky.

When we finished, one of the jeep drivers made an announcement:

"This is where you get off. These men," he gestured toward the armed group, "will take you the rest of the way to Tripoli. Beyond this point, it gets dangerous. But these men will protect you."

Lover Boy raised the obvious question.

"Do we need to pay them separately? We've already paid you for Tripoli."

The driver smiled and shook his head.

"No, you don't owe them anything. We've paid them. This is part of the arrangement. Don't worry—just follow their lead and you'll reach Tripoli safely."

We began unloading our belongings from the jeep.

The armed men and their leader had already driven back uphill to where their other vehicles and men were stationed.

Once all our bags were on the ground, the driver gave us one last favor—a second refill of our water bottles. It was a small mercy. That evening, we had plenty of water.

The sun was setting by the time the jeep that brought us drove away, leaving us behind on the rocky path.

From where I stood, I could see men up on the hill—guns slung over their shoulders, silhouetted by the fading light, watching us.

After Maghreb prayer, one of the jeeps up on the hill drove down toward us.

As it rumbled closer, we instinctively gathered near our belongings.

Two armed men stepped out.

One of them, tall and sharp-eyed, came forward and made a quick announcement:

"We are not going anywhere tonight. Camp here. We leave early in the morning."

Before anyone could ask a single question, the two men were back in their jeep, heading uphill again—just as quickly as they had come.

We stood there, unsure what to make of it, watching their taillights disappear into the darkening slope.

Arrogant Girl was the first to speak.

"We never came here to camp," she snapped at Lover Boy. "Why didn't you tell them we want to continue the journey?"

As usual, Lover Boy didn't respond. He just looked at the ground.

It was Ayesha who replied instead.

"It's not up to us to decide when to leave or stay."

Everyone in our group nodded silently. No one was going to argue with that.

Still, I couldn't stop thinking about those men—their cold faces, the way their hands rested on their weapons. Something didn't feel right.

I kept the feeling to myself.

Later, after Isha, we gathered and shared the last of our food. Our water was low. Our provisions were nearly gone. Ahmed and some others hoped we'd be resupplied in the morning by these new "guides."

But Quiet Girl voiced what many were thinking.

"Those people seem... hostile."

Hafiz, always the optimist, tried to reassure her.

"The driver said they carry weapons for our protection. We have nothing to fear."

Lover Boy spoke for the first time since Arrogant Girl's jab.

"But what if it's not for our protection? What if they decide to use them on us? What would we do then?"

Arrogant Girl didn't let the chance slip.

"You can protect us—all the women. Like a man," she said sarcastically. "That's what you'll do, right? Except you probably don't have the courage. You can't even go ask for food or water."

There was silence. Lover Boy didn't reply right away. When he finally did, it was in a low, trembling voice:

"I will protect you... trust me." He lowered his head. I could see his shoulders shaking. He was crying.

That didn't stop Arrogant Girl. "Then go. Talk to them. Ask when we're leaving. We paid for this journey. Food and water are our right."

Lover Boy slowly got to his feet. But Hafiz, sitting beside him, gently pulled him back down.

"What rights are you talking about?" he said to her. "We have no rights here. Still, I believe those men are here to protect us. Like the driver said."

The argument carried on—mostly between Arrogant Girl and Hafiz. The rest of us grew quiet. Ahmed and Quiet Girl had already fallen asleep, curled under their jackets.

I turned toward Ayesha, who was staring at me, as if waiting for me to say something.

"Go to the bathroom now," I whispered. "I'm not helping you in the middle of the night."

She didn't say a word—just smiled softly and tucked her face between her knees.

The next day, soon after Fajr prayer, two jeeps rolled down the hill. The drivers got out and told us to load our things and get on board.

"What about some water and breakfast?" Lover Boy asked hesitantly.

One of them shot back, "You'll get it later. We need to leave now—security problem."

Without further explanation, our caravan of three jeeps set off before sunrise.

The leader rode in the first vehicle with two armed guards and a third man we later learned was his younger brother.

This time, with fewer passengers per jeep—about fifteen to twenty—we were at least spared the discomfort of having our legs dangling in the air.

We assumed there'd be a break within an hour or so. But time dragged on. Every time someone asked to stop, or pleaded for water, the driver repeated the same two words: "Security problem."

By late afternoon, our mouths were dry, our stomachs empty, and our energy gone.

Finally, the jeeps came to a halt and we were told we'd stay the night and continue further the next morning.

"We'll bring water and food," one of them said before they drove off and parked a distance away.

We collapsed on the sand, drained of strength. No one had the will to speak—we just stared at the horizon, waiting.

"Let's offer our Asr prayer. It's time," said Hafiz, getting to his feet.

Just after Asr, one jeep approached.

They handed out two small bottles of water to each of us and promised food later.

Most of us drained at least one bottle right away.

"Be careful with the water. It's short here," Ayesha warned, her voice calm but commanding.

She looked graceful even in exhaustion.

I felt a deep pity for her—and for all the women—enduring this journey with quiet dignity.

Then Ayesha made a suggestion. "We should appoint someone to manage our water. To ration it wisely."

She nominated me. Everyone agreed.

That day, I became the custodian of our drinking water—a role far more difficult than it sounded. Every drop now passed through my hands.

After Maghreb, we saw headlights in the distance. A jeep came with our dinner: plain boiled rice, served into our bare hands—two handfuls each.

No plates. No spoons. Just warm grains steaming in the dusk air.

No one refused.

We sat and ate in silence.

"We leave early tomorrow," they told us, then drove off again.

Later, as we huddled after Isha prayer, Arrogant Girl voiced her disgust. "The way they served us food—like animals."

No one replied.

We were beyond arguing about what we couldn't control.

That night, we were all startled awake by the cold. The wind cut through our clothes. I was wearing everything I had and still couldn't stop shivering.

"We need to dig a trench," Hafiz announced.

"Dig a trench? What do you mean?" Ayesha asked, rising slowly.

Hafiz explained: "The sand will shield us from the wind and trap our body heat. It's all we've got."

The idea sounded crazy, but also logical.

So we began.

With our bare hands, we dug. The ground was soft but the work was slow. We managed to dig about a foot deep, and the sand we piled up around it gave us another foot of wall.

It took nearly an hour, but when we climbed inside the trench and sat close together, leaning against the sides, it worked. The cold no longer gnawed at our bones.

The next morning, I woke up for Fajr prayer and noticed Ayesha sleeping very close to me.

She was holding the end of my shirt in her hand.

My movements stirred her awake.

She slowly let go of the fabric.

We didn't say a word.

By then, the rest of our group had also woken up, and we all climbed out of the trench together.

As we had done every day, we left before sunrise, driving deeper into the desert.

Hour after hour, the jeeps sped through an endless sea of sand, heading toward lands we didn't know.

For the next three days, the routine was unchanged.

Image Credits: AI generated image by Malick Mahmood

That night, we were all startled awake by the cold. "We need to dig a trench," Hafiz announced, "The sand will shield us from the wind and trap our body heat. It's all we've got."

Food and water came once every twenty-four hours, around Maghreb—two handfuls of plain boiled rice and a refill of our bottles.

We had all silently agreed: no complaints, no questions. Just endurance.

On what must have been our fifth or sixth day, we finally saw people in the distance—faint silhouettes on the horizon.

Excitement spread through our group.

"It could be Tripoli," someone said.

For a brief moment, I allowed myself to believe it too.

Our jeeps slowed and stopped nearby.

Before we could climb down, the people rushed toward us, begging for water—their eyes wild, their voices desperate.

"Yallah! Yallah!" the drivers and guards shouted, signaling us to offload quickly.

Then it turned chaotic.

The people who had arrived before us lunged for our water. As the custodian, I had to act fast.

With help from Ahmed and Ayesha, I managed to stash away our bottles before they could be snatched.

The drivers didn't intervene.

They just waited until we were all off the jeeps. Then they drove off a short distance and got out.

What happened next made our blood run cold. They began aerial firing, shots ringing out over the desert sky.

It wasn't a warning. It was a celebration.

They laughed.

They shouted.

They fired again and again—like they'd just achieved something big.

We just stood there, stunned.

Image Credits: AI generated image by Malick Mahmood

We finally saw people in the distance—faint silhouettes on the horizon. Excitement spread through our group. "It could be Tripoli," someone said. For a brief moment, I allowed myself to believe it too.

Nobody moved.
Nobody spoke.
Confusion clouded every face.
But in my gut, I felt the truth.

I looked around—sick, hungry, and thirsty people already there before us. Eyes that had seen too much. Bodies that barely held together.

I could feel my heart pounding loud, matching the clatter of gunfire.

And then, there in the middle of nowhere, somewhere in the Sahara Desert, I asked myself a question I had feared for days:

"Have we been kidnapped?"

Sahara Desert to Sabha, Libya

"Did you see that, Yousuf?" Ahmed whispered, his voice trembling.

He was still staring at the gunfire.

Ayesha, standing next to him, looked stunned.

"We've been taken hostage," I said quietly, but with certainty.

There was no point pretending anymore.

As our group clustered together, the fear on every face was unmistakable.

"But how could they do that?" Arrogant Girl blurted out, her voice shrill. "We've already paid for our travel expenses!"

Lover Boy answered before anyone else could.

"They can do it because they have guns."

Everyone started talking at once—murmurs, panic, rising voices.

A helpless chorus.

I looked off toward our captors.

Their tents stood firm in the sand—too solid, too settled.

This wasn't temporary.

We weren't moving anytime soon.

"Water, do you have water? I need water!" Someone grabbed my shoulder.

I turned to see a man with baggy pants, one hand awkwardly holding them up.

There was something comical about him, and despite everything, I smiled.

Later, we started calling him Waterman, because he always asked for water.

He didn't waste time sugar-coating things.

"I've been here over a month," he said. "These pants used to fit me when I got here."

Then he told us the truth.

The full, bitter truth.

Stories of hunger.

Neglect.

Punishment.

Waiting endlessly in the heat with nothing but hope drying out in your throat.

Ayesha turned to him. "But… is there any way to get out of this?"

Waterman gave a small, bitter laugh and gestured toward the tents. "If you can pay the ransom, yes."

Her face stiffened. "And if someone doesn't have the money?"

His voice went cold.

"Then they'll let you rot right here. In the middle of nowhere." He spread his arms wide to emphasize the endless wilderness of the Sahara Desert.

It looked like hell, and we were already inside it.

Meanwhile, I noticed a stir in our captors' camp. A jeep sped toward us, carrying four or five armed men.

Waterman suddenly stood up, alarmed.

"Do as they say. Don't argue. If you misbehave, they'll shoot you in the head."

I frowned.

For a moment, it felt like he was helping them, trying to scare us into submission. But before I could say anything, he added softly:

"I'm not trying to scare you more than necessary. Just want you to know what they're capable of. Take it as advice… from a friend."

Then he went quiet.

The jeep had stopped.

The men jumped out—faces hard, rifles slung across their chests.

One unfolded a chair and placed it carefully in the sand. Their leader stepped forward and sat, while another man held an umbrella over him.

We, the kidnapped, were ordered to sit on the scorching sand, with no shade.

Even though the sun had started going down, the heat still clung to the ground, seeping into our skin.

We gathered around.

"Four hundred dollars each for those who pay now," the leader announced. "One thousand if you get it wired from back home."

His name was Ahmed, and I'd never forget it.

A second man—tall, broad-shouldered, with a coiled rage beneath his skin—spoke next.

"We bought you for a good price. Now we want our money back." His name was Ali, Ahmed's younger brother.

They were both Muslims—at least by name.

But names are just labels.

Islam isn't inherited like skin or eye color.

It's a way of life.

These men lived by none of its teachings.

"But we already paid for the journey. How can you ask for more?" Someone from the back dared to speak.

Ali didn't answer. He pointed at the man.

"Come here."

The man obeyed, hesitant.

Waterman leaned toward me. "Poor guy… they'll kill him."

Ali slapped him—hard.

Then others joined in, punching, kicking, stomping him into the ground.

One unfolded a chair and placed it carefully in the sand. Their leader stepped forward and sat, while another man held an umbrella over him. We, the kidnapped, were ordered to sit on the scorching sand, with no shade.

The desert went silent, except for the sounds of fists and pain.

I didn't wait.

I dug into my pouch and began counting our money.

I didn't want any trouble for Ahmed or myself.

"Does anybody else have any questions?" Ahmed's voice rang out, cold and sarcastic.

I foolishly raised my hand.

His eyes locked onto mine.

"So you, too, have a question?"

"No, no, Sir. You got me wrong." I quickly lowered my hand. "I only wanted to ask—where do I pay… for myself and my friend?"

He stared at me for a moment.

Then, without a word, he beckoned me forward.

I handed him eight hundred dollars.

Ali opened a register and wrote down our names.

I was the first to pay that day. A few others followed soon after.

Lover Boy had some cash but not enough for two. He chose to pay for Arrogant Girl, not for himself. There was no need to ask why. It was obvious.

For those who didn't have the money, Ahmed the leader gave clear instructions. "You'll get one chance to make a phone call using the satellite phone. One. When you get connected, don't waste time—just tell them to call back. Think carefully about who you'll call. There won't be a second chance."

It was almost Maghreb time when Ahmed and his men returned to their tents.

The ones who had to make phone calls were told they'd do it the next day.

After prayers, they handed out our food and water.

We were told to line up with our bottles, which they refilled from a dusty blue container.

Then they gave us dinner: two handfuls of cold, tasteless, boiled rice.

No salt.

No oil.

No kindness.

That night, we huddled again in our shallow trench. Waterman was now part of our group. There were eight, maybe nine of us.

It was quiet.

Just the occasional breeze across the sand and the distant laughter of our captors.

Ahmed, sitting on my right, leaned forward slightly and asked: "Ayesha, who do you think you'll call?"

She was on my left.

Her voice came softly in the darkness.

"I… I really don't know."

I couldn't see her face, but I could hear the fear in her voice—thin, trembling, uncertain.

She was scared.

We all were.

I could have helped Ayesha if I'd had the enough money to buy her out of this hell.

"Did you notice the water they're giving us has fuel in it?" Waterman raised another issue, but most people didn't respond. Everyone had more immediate concerns. Still, I listened—because I knew what it meant to drink water laced with gasoline.

"It's not safe," I warned our group. "Drink as little as possible. Just wet your lips if you must."

The next morning, our captors returned with two lists— one for those who had paid, and another for those allowed to make a phone call.

They seemed to take pride in humiliating us, as if stripping us of dignity would make us easier to manage.

Then I heard Ali call out:

"Come here, Ayesha. Who you want to call?"

She walked up to them slowly.

One of the armed men whistled crudely as she passed. Ahmed the leader looked her up and down with predatory amusement.

"Who would you like to call, Beauty?" he asked, eyes gleaming. "Do you have someone back home who can pay for you?"

Ayesha stared at the ground, silent.

Her posture was small, shrinking.

Ahmed stepped closer. "No one? Hm." Then with a mocking smile, he shoved her lightly. "Go. We shall deal with you later."

Ayesha came back and sat beside me, more shaken than before.

She didn't say a word, but I could feel her trembling.

That day, some got their one chance to call family back home.

Some calls didn't go through.

Others had no one left to call.

And a few—like Ayesha and Quiet Girl—simply didn't know who to call.

That evening, a young man died of malaria.

Waterman told us he was from Ethiopia, had fallen ill shortly after arriving. His father had actually paid for his return.

"Then why didn't they send him back?" Arrogant Girl asked.

"Because they were waiting for someone going that way to take him," Waterman replied.

After Asr, we prayed the Janaza for him and buried him in the sand.

The next morning after Fajr, I drifted back to sleep.

When I woke up, the sun was already beating down on the trench.

It was unbearable.

Ayesha and Ahmed were gone.

I climbed out and scanned the camp.

All I could see was despair. It felt like a place people had been gathered just to rot in the burning sand.

Then I saw them returning—Ahmed and Ayesha walking slowly toward me.

"We went for a little stroll," Ahmed said.

He looked hollow.

Ayesha's face was pale and tight with fear.

"Yousuf... do you know what we saw?" Ayesha said quietly. "There are dead bodies over there. Half-buried in sand."

"That's just one graveyard you saw," Waterman's voice came from behind. "There are many of them... all around us."

Ayesha's voice cracked. "Can't we at least give them a proper burial?" She probably didn't know what else to say. Maybe she just needed to believe that some dignity could still exist in this place.

Then I noticed Ahmed sitting on the ground, gulping water from his bottle.

I rushed over, startled.

"Slow down. That water's contaminated—it could make you sick." I gently took the bottle from him.

His eyes were filled with something darker than fear.

A quiet hopelessness.

"Yousuf, what has life ever given us—except pain? I wish our leaders back home could see us now."

And then the tears came.

Silent at first.

Then steady.

I knelt beside him.

"Ahmed, remember why we're here. For our families. We're walking through hell so they can live in peace. Our sacrifice will mean something... it has to."

I wasn't sure if he believed me.

I wasn't even sure if I believed me.

But in that moment, words were all we had.

On our third day, the smugglers ordered the remaining refugees—those who hadn't yet paid—to make one final call to anyone who might send ransom money.

Ayesha still had no one to call.

I tried, without success, to collect money for her.

Her situation was beginning to gnaw at me. I had already decided to give her my last dollars, hoping it might help, even if only a little.

Later that day, when they called her to the front again, every pair of eyes among the captors turned to her.

Ahmed, their leader, was watching her intently.

She seemed to sense what was coming.

Like before, she stood silently, staring at her feet.

Ahmed, the leader didn't care about her silence.

With a smirk, he leaned forward and said loud enough for everyone to hear, "You could always join me in my tent. Earn your way out."

The words hit her like a slap.

Ayesha's face flushed—bright and furious—as she walked back to where I was sitting.

I lowered my voice and said, "Ayesha, I wish we could do something for you."

"This isn't a movie," she replied coldly, still fuming. "Only in movies does the hero save the day."

I hesitated, then asked, "Why didn't you arrange for the ransom before starting this journey?"

"How could I have planned for this?" she snapped, then softened. "Nobody tells you this part."

"What about your family? You could call them, couldn't you?"

"All the people who might've helped are angry at me for leaving without a word. And I only remember one phone number…"

I leaned in. "Whose number?"

"My father's," she said, her voice almost a whisper. "And I don't want to call him."

"Why not? He's your father. I'm sure he'll help you out of this—out of whatever this is."

"I'll think about it."

"Don't just think. Tomorrow, when they call you again, give them his number."

She didn't respond.

That day, the tension shifted.

Some people, those who had received callbacks from home with confirmed payments, looked visibly relieved. For a few, the hope of freedom was back.

After Asr prayer, complaints about the gasoline in our drinking water grew louder.

Most agreed we had to speak to them about it.

"They should at least treat those differently who've already paid," Arrogant Girl argued, trying to reason with the absurd.

I stayed out of the debate.

I had no interest in demanding anything from our captors. But my friend Ahmed disagreed.

He insisted on joining the group that would go to their tents to negotiate.

Just before Maghreb, Ahmed, Lover Boy, and two others set out to speak with the smugglers.

The rest of us waited, tense and silent, watching them walk into the heat-hazed distance.

The tents were farther away than we'd thought.

The only thing they wanted to discuss was the water. We weren't asking for much—just that they stop giving us poison. We agreed to take one bottle a day instead of two, if only it meant that the water would be clean.

First, we saw a man step out of the tent.

He stood there for a few seconds while our negotiating party spoke to him.

Then he turned, went back inside, and re-emerged with several other men—all armed.

Without a word, they began hitting and kicking our people.

One of them splashed a liquid—probably gasoline—on Ahmed and the others as they fell to the ground.

Their leader was yelling like a madman, "Burn them! Burn them!"

Panic erupted.

Somehow, our group broke free and started running back toward us.

The smugglers fired bullets into the sand around their feet, missing only by inches.

My heart pounded so loud I could hear it in my ears. None of us could help them—except pray.

I kept my eyes on Ahmed.

Bullets kicked up sand near him as he sprinted with what little energy he had left.

Panting and gasping, they made it back.

The smell of gasoline clung to them like death.

"They were going to burn us," Lover Boy cried out, clearly in shock.

I threw my arms around Ahmed and muttered, "I told you not to go to those animals."

"I was so scared," he said, shivering.

He was crying.

That incident shattered whatever illusion anyone still held—that these captors had a shred of humanity.

Each day, we battled the blazing sun, and each night, we froze under the stars.

A few more people managed to pay their ransoms. But Ayesha and Quiet Girl still couldn't.

One day, they did give some phone numbers to Ahmed the leader, hoping for a miracle.

But the numbers didn't work.

Either they were wrong or disconnected.

From then on, Ahmed began harassing Ayesha openly. His comments were filthy, degrading.

She started hiding from him at night, too frightened to sleep.

"I'm scared I'll die out here in the desert," she whispered to me once.

Her voice trembled.

I didn't know what to say.

They had cleared it to us that we would only be moved once thirty people had paid. But nearly two weeks had passed, and only eighteen had.

No one was going anywhere.

We had already buried three men and one woman. They had all died the same way—sudden vomiting of blood followed by death within two days.

We all knew what was killing them: the contaminated water.

I chose thirst over poison, but it was taking its toll.

I was weak, dizzy, and dehydrated.

We were in a miserable state—no clean water, barely any food, nowhere to sleep, and no hope.

During our third week in captivity, my friend Ahmed fell ill.

We had just finished offering our Fajr prayer when he started coughing.

He pulled his hand away from his mouth—and it was stained with blood.

That night, his condition worsened.

I cradled his head in my lap, gently massaging his forehead as we spoke about our journey and the dreams that had carried us this far.

"Yousuf, I don't think I'll be able to continue," he said softly, his eyes filled with despair.

"No, brother. You will make it. We'll reach the other side—nothing can stop us," I replied, trying to sound strong and determined.

But I think Ahmed saw the doubt in my eyes too.

I stayed awake all night, holding him as he lay there, growing weaker.

Our friends gathered around, praying for him.

Hafiz recited Qur'an through the dark hours, his voice trembling.

"Yousuf, if you make it to the peaceful lands, and you get the chance to talk with my family, tell them I tried to change their lives... but I failed," Ahmed whispered.

He knew he was dying.

"You're going to recover, my friend. We'll enter those lands together," I told him, because what else could I say?

I wished, in that moment, our leaders, our politicians, the powerful people back home, could see what I was seeing: a teenage boy dying in my arms.

What would they have done if it were their son lying there instead of Ahmed?

He kept repeating his regrets, his apologies. I saw tears forming in his dry eyes.

I feared if I cried, my tears would turn to blood—because we were so dehydrated. When one tear finally fell onto Ahmed's forehead, I stared at it, unsure if it was water or blood.

It looked like blood.

By the next afternoon, Ahmed's condition had worsened.

He slipped in and out of consciousness.

His body burned with fever, and we had nothing cold to ease his pain.

Many of our fellow travelers had gathered around him, sadness etched into their faces.

As Asr prayer approached, Ahmed turned to me and asked for water.

"Ahmed, my brother… this water is no good. It'll make you worse," I warned.

But he kept pleading.

Finally, I gave in.

I brought over the bottle and poured water gently into his open mouth.

He took three or four large gulps… then started coughing violently, spitting up blood.

That day, while someone made the Adhan for Asr prayer, my friend—my brother, my companion—breathed his last in my arms.

Ahmed died.

May God bless his soul.

I just sat there, holding him.

Silent tears streamed down my face.

All the years we had spent together flashed before my eyes. I remembered how excited he had been to leave Somalia, chasing a dream of a better life for himself and his family.

He was not even eighteen.

He died in the desert, a victim of the smugglers' cruelty and greed. They had already taken so many young lives. And I have no doubt—they will burn in hell for it.

Waterman, Hafiz, and a few others came to console me.

Everyone knew Ahmed had been my closest friend.

"It was his destiny," Ayesha said through her tears.

Some of the men carried his body to the area where we had left the others who had died.

We had gotten used to it by then—when someone died, we carried them a little farther into the desert and left them to the mercy of the wind.

The desert always buried them.

Those preparing for Asr invited me to join.

Hafiz announced we would offer Janaza for Ahmed afterward.

Something inside me broke that day.

After Ahmed's death, I began drinking the same water that had killed him.

Ayesha and the others watched me silently, as if they were already mourning again—only this time, for me.

From that moment on, I stopped caring.

I drank all the water our captors gave us.

Most of the time, I just sat there, staring at the spot where Ahmed's body had been.

I couldn't believe he was gone.

It looked like he was just sleeping, and any moment now he'd wake up and come to me.

On the cold nights, when sleep refused to come, I would remember him and quietly cry.

A few days after Ahmed's death, someone asked me if another person could now travel in his place.

Ayesha came to mind.

But before we could even bring it up with the captors, Ahmed the leader made it clear—no one would be allowed to take the place of someone who had paid and later died.

It took several days of sandstorms to finally bury my friend.

Nature did what we could not.

Ahmed was gone.

By then, I had grown so weak I could barely lift my head.

Ahmed the leader continued to show up with his brother and their guards.

They would kick and beat us, sometimes throwing fuel in our faces.

They jeered at the women, offering them a place in their tents as sex slaves—for fifty dollars a month.

"All those who haven't paid can rot here in the desert," they laughed cruelly.

As always, the leader focused his cruelty on Ayesha.

One day he grabbed her by the hair and dragged her toward me.

"Look! Your girlfriend!" he mocked. "Come on, get up and save her!"

He couldn't begin to understand the lifelessness in our bodies.

We were too weak even to be humiliated.

That night, I sat with my head buried between my knees. I didn't want to see anything anymore.

Then I felt a hand slide gently behind my back.

It was Ayesha's.

She was trying to pull me toward her, as if to hug me.

For a moment, I wished she were my mother—so I could break down and cry on her shoulder, let everything go.

"Yousuf," she whispered, "I wish I could do something for you... or at least fill the space Ahmed left behind."

I lifted my head and looked at her.

I thought to myself, this poor girl couldn't even fill the seat Ahmed vacated when he died—and yet she wanted to fill the void in my heart.

That night, we heard music and laughter coming from the smugglers' tents.

A rumor was going around: a female traveler had agreed to work for them and had moved into their tents.

Under those circumstances, no one could judge whether she was right or wrong.

Around noon the next day, I began feeling dizzy.

A sharp, stabbing pain twisted through my stomach.

The last thought that crossed my mind before I collapsed was of my own death.

When I opened my eyes, I saw Ayesha.

My head was resting in her lap, and she was crying.

I could hear Hafiz softly reciting Qur'an.

A crowd had gathered around me—men and women, many of them girls.

For a moment, I thought I had died and they were mourning me. But then I felt Ayesha's tears land on my cheeks.

I was alive.

She told me later that I had been unconscious for two days.

The next morning, after I had recovered somewhat, a new group arrived—thirty or forty men and women. People rushed toward them, fighting for food and water. Just one sip of clean, fresh water—untainted by gasoline—felt like a miracle.

Waterman came to me and said, "They're going to take us out of here soon."

I was surprised. He hadn't even joined the chaos for water.

"How do you know?" I asked.

He nodded toward the new group. "Some of them will pay right away. That'll get us to the number they want."

Late the next morning, Ahmed the leader arrived and repeated the same speech he'd given when we first arrived.

Sure enough, several people from the new group paid on the spot.

Waterman was right—we were finally close to the required thirty.

After Asr prayer, the smugglers called everyone to gather.

Ahmed the leader stood before us and announced that we would be leaving the next day. Thirty people had paid to travel to Tripoli.

A wave of joy spread through those who had secured a place. For the rest, a heavy desperation set in.

Once the captors left, people began greeting and congratulating one another.

That night, I took out all the money I had and handed it to Ayesha.

She refused at first. "I can't take this from you."

But I insisted until she accepted it.

"Yousuf," she said softly, "I'll give you my father's phone number. If you ever get the chance, please call him. Tell him where I am and what he needs to do to get me out of here."

She shifted closer to me.

The warmth of her body helped fight off the cold, but it didn't stir any excitement in me—it was comfort, nothing more.

We stayed up all night talking.

Much of our conversation circled back to Ahmed, my friend.

We were still talking about him when we heard Hafiz make call for Fajr prayer which echoed across the desert.

After Fajr prayer, I walked over to the place where we had buried Ahmed.

I sat there for a long time, praying for him.

The sun had already risen by the time I stood up.

A jeep, much like the one that had brought us here, rumbled toward the camp.

Everyone gathered around it.

Soon, Ahmed the leader and his men arrived in another vehicle.

The first thing he did was call Ayesha and Quiet Girl to him. He spoke to them privately.

Neither of them replied—they just stood there, eyes downcast, helpless as ever.

Then Ali barked an order for the thirty people who had paid to form a line and prepare to board the jeep.

Ayesha lifted her head and looked directly at me.

Our eyes locked for a long, silent moment before someone behind me pushed forward, breaking the connection.

It was then I realized people were lining up.

I stayed back to board last—I wanted to sit at the edge, away from the center.

The women had already started boarding, as usual taking the middle section. We had been there for more than a month. In that time, we had lost some of our companions. Now we were leaving behind others who were still clinging to life.

I found my place—last seat on the left side of the jeep. Waterman sat to my right.

In the distance, I could see Lover Boy waving at us. Ayesha still stood beside the leader. Behind her was the place where Ahmed was buried.

The engine roared to life.

At that moment, Ayesha looked up and locked eyes with me again.

We stared at each other as the jeep gave a little jerk and began to roll out.

As we moved forward, the propelling sand behind us began to blur everything. It swallowed the view of those left behind—Ayesha, the others, even Ahmed's resting place. It was as though the desert itself had begun to bury the living, just as it had the dead.

The day turned into night, but we kept driving. We wondered if the next destination would bring an end to our suffering—or simply begin another chapter of torment. It was well past midnight when we finally stopped, and the driver told us we'd rest there for the night.

Once they got us off the jeep, the smugglers drove away, as usual. They always slept far from us, perhaps out of fear.

I didn't feel like speaking to anyone, so I stepped away to make up the prayers I had missed during the journey.

The night was bitterly cold. I couldn't sleep, not for a minute. My mind churned with thoughts and memories I couldn't silence.

By morning, I was the first one standing, though my body was shivering.

A young girl from the newest group came over and handed me a short-sleeve jacket. "It's a spare—you can have it," she said kindly. She was traveling with an old woman, and both had paid their ransom immediately after joining us. Since we departed the next day, we hadn't had the chance to know them well.

It was late in the morning when the jeep returned.

We climbed in, taking our usual spots.

Again, we were swallowed by endless sand, with only the blazing sun glaring down from above.

About an hour into the journey, the jeep hit a bump—and Waterman went flying off. He tumbled across the sand like a rag doll. We banged on the jeep bed, shouting until the driver finally stopped.

I was the first to reach Waterman, who lay motionless on the sand, one hand still gripping his pants. Everyone crowded around him, trying to revive him, but he looked completely out of it.

I sprinkled water on his face.

"Water… please… water," he murmured.

I held my bottle to his lips and he drank deeply.

Just then, the two armed guards with us approached, shouting. Without warning, they began kicking Waterman. Amazingly, he shot to his feet and sprinted back to the jeep.

It was almost comical.

Just moments earlier, he seemed half-dead. But two kicks from the guards brought him fully back to life.

Soon we were all back on board and moving again.

"Hold on tight, my friend," I told him.

He nodded, still catching his breath.

We traveled like that—jeep, sand, sun, and brief rest periods—for three more grueling days and nights. The desert felt never-ending, a nightmare painted in beige and heat.

My legs, from the hips down, had gone completely numb.

Just before nightfall on the third day, we arrived at a checkpoint. Uniformed men stood guard. They looked like military personnel—Chadian, I guessed.

We were ordered off the jeep and made to stand in a line. Guns pointed at us, they began yelling in a language we didn't understand.

"They're going to shoot us!" someone cried out.

Our driver explained that unless we paid them, they'd open fire.

"But how can we pay?" Hafiz protested. "We've been in the desert for more than a month. Where would we get money from?"

Then Arrogant Girl approached me. "The old woman traveling with the girl who gave you the jacket," she said, "I think she has some money."

We rushed to the old woman and pleaded with her. The young girl also begged on our behalf. Finally, the old woman nodded.

"I have one hundred dollars left," she said, "but I'll only give it to Yousuf. I want my money back once we reach the city."

I was stunned. Why me?

"I only trust Yousuf," she added. "He'll return it."

"Take it, Yousuf," Waterman said. "We'll repay her when we get to the city. We'll find a way—call home if we must."

Everyone agreed.

With great reluctance, I accepted the money from her and walked over to the driver.

"This is all we have," I told him.

The armed men wanted more, but the driver convinced them we were truly out of funds. After some tense negotiation, they accepted the hundred dollars—and allowed us to pass.

After we passed that checkpoint, we drove for another two days before reaching a small, hilly area. The driver stopped the jeep, and we all climbed off. I collapsed onto the sand, exhausted. Needing a moment of solitude, I crawled a few steps away from the group to offer my prayers.

Even before I could finish, I heard the sound of an approaching vehicle. My heart sank—I thought it might be military or some government force coming to arrest us. But when I glanced over at the driver and his men, they looked calm, even casual.

Moments later, a large flatbed jeep rolled into view. One of the guards who had traveled with us stood up and made an announcement: from that point onward, we would be transferred to this new jeep. It would take us to the port of Tripoli.

We boarded the second vehicle just as the sun was dipping below the horizon. This new driver, unlike the others, wasn't armed. That alone felt like a small relief.

We traveled for another day and a half until we reached a farmhouse in the middle of nowhere.

There, we found a water pump—an actual, functioning water pump. It felt like we had stumbled upon a miracle.

We fell upon it like thirsty animals. Though our stomachs were full, our throats couldn't get enough of that cool, clean water. We drank until we were drenched inside and out, then laughed and played like children.

For the first time in what felt like ages, I smelled the pure scent of fresh water.

The driver soon returned with some chicken and rice. "You'll find some utensils in the kitchen," he said. "Take this and cook yourselves a meal."

It felt unreal—having food, water, and even the faint comfort of a roof.

After eating, the driver told us he'd return in the morning to take us to the city.

That night, worn out and full, we fell into a deep, dreamless sleep.

The following morning, we once again rushed to the water pump. Everyone drank as much as they could, and a few even sat beneath it to take a quick bath. It felt like a luxury.

Later that morning, the driver arrived—this time with an additional jeep.

We were divided into two groups.

Waterman and Arrogant Girl ended up in the other vehicle.

After about six hours of driving, we reached a paved road. It was the first time in what felt like forever that we had seen real asphalt—a true road. To us, it was more than just concrete; it was a symbol of life and civilization. We all assumed we must be close to a city—probably Tripoli.

We stayed on that paved road for around thirty minutes before the jeeps turned off and veered into the desert again. Another hour of off-road driving brought us to a small grove of trees.

The drivers let us out to rest.

As we sat in the shade, trying to cool down, we suddenly heard engines approaching.

Panic set in.

Some people even tried to hide behind the trees.

Four more vehicles arrived—these looked more like mini-buses, with proper seats and windows. The drivers told us we would now be transferred into these jeeps for the final leg of the journey to the city.

We set off around Asr time.

The sun was still high when we arrived at a military checkpoint.

"Libyan army," our driver muttered.

Fear returned to our faces.

We warned the driver we had no money to bribe anyone this time. But fortunately, after a short conversation between one of our drivers and the soldiers, we were waved through without trouble.

Roughly two hours later, we finally entered a city. The driver announced, "This is Sabha, Libya."

It felt like we had returned to the world of the living. It had been so long since we'd seen streets, buildings, signs of human life. We navigated through broken, dusty roads before arriving at a house located in the middle of a large open area. Our convoy stopped and we got out in a rush, filled with cautious excitement. People were smiling again. It really felt like our journey might be coming to an end.

The drivers led us inside the house and directed us into a large room.

"You can rest here tonight," one of them said. "Tomorrow, new jeeps will come to take you to the port of Tripoli. From there, you'll sail to Italy."

As he walked out, I sat down, uneasy.

Something about the house made me uncomfortable. I didn't know what it was—I just wasn't ready to trust the people who had brought us here.

"Welcome to Libya, my friend," Waterman said, patting me on the back.

I gave him a faint smile, but my heart remained heavy.

Image Credits: AI generated image by Malick Mahmood

We had arrived in Libya during a time of deep unrest. The government had been overthrown, nearly everyone was armed, and chaos seemed to rule the land. Almost every other house belonged to a gang of human traffickers.

Sabha to Tripoli

We had arrived in Libya during a time of deep unrest. The government had been overthrown, nearly everyone was armed, and chaos seemed to rule the land.

"Although humans are the superior creation, we can't just fly across countries like birds," Hafiz said quietly, his tone laced with sadness.

The expression on his face mirrored the insecurity I felt within myself.

Waterman, however, was in high spirits—perhaps because he had spent even longer in the desert and knew that, at the very least, we were moving forward.

Being around Hafiz and Waterman reminded me of my friend Ahmed.

I was still lost in thoughts of him and how he died when the door to our room burst open with a loud thud.

A large man entered, holding a metal chain dripping with blood.

Behind him were a group of young boys—no older than sixteen or seventeen—bleeding and crying, some of them soaked in urine.

They were followed by three more heavyset Libyan men, each holding either chains or iron rods.

Panic swept through the room like a wave.

It became instantly clear: we were in serious trouble once again.

The Libyans didn't say a word.

They exited through the front door, which they locked behind them, leaving us in stunned silence.

Waterman shrank into a corner, his face pale.

Hafiz, calm but concerned, approached the bleeding boys and spoke to them softly.

They were from Somalia, Nigeria, Eritrea, Ethiopia, Pakistan and Sudan. Like us, they were refugees hoping to get to Europe—but were instead captured and locked inside this house, now used as a private prison.

"What do they want from us?" Waterman asked in a trembling voice.

"Fifteen hundred U.S. dollars—each," came the grim reply from a Somali boy who sat beside me.

He told me he had already escaped from one Libyan prison only to be caught by another group of captors. "Most of these big houses you see around here," he said, "are prisons where Libyans keep people like us to demand ransom."

By Isha time, more refugees were brought in—including some familiar faces from our desert group.

At first, I didn't know what had happened to the women who had travelled with us. But that night, they marched us out to a courtyard for dinner, and I saw some of them.

The old woman and her daughter were there—but not Arrogant Girl.

We were served boiled rice with a bit of tomato and onion. It tasted like a feast after all we had endured. But just as we began to eat, a Libyan man—clearly the leader—entered the courtyard with a team of armed guards.

Without warning, they began hitting and kicking us.

We scattered, backing away toward the walls in fear.

"He looks like their boss," Waterman whispered beside me.

The man made a chilling announcement.

Each of us, he declared, would have to pay fifteen hundred U.S. dollars for our freedom.

He claimed he had bought us from our previous captors and now wanted to double his investment.

"Those who don't pay," he shouted, "will rot to death in here."

The beatings continued as they exited the courtyard, but I managed to avoid them that day by not being in their path.

Later, we sat around discussing what little we knew.

"What happens if someone can't pay?" Waterman asked the question that was on everyone's mind.

A man we didn't know answered, "Tomorrow you'll be allowed one phone call home. If the money doesn't arrive in a day or two, they'll beat you twice as hard."

The next morning, after a pitiful breakfast of dry bread and water, the leader returned with his guards.

As before, they kicked and beat us before making the same announcement: pay now or make your one phone call.

"Be careful who you call," the Somali boy whispered again. "If the money doesn't come, they punish you even more."

I knew there was no way I could ask my parents for that kind of money. I had to face this alone, no matter what it cost me.

Just then, the old woman stood up.

Her daughter remained seated.

The woman suddenly pointed a finger at me. "I gave all my money to Yousuf," she shouted, then turned to the leader and begged him to retrieve her money.

Everyone froze.

Even her daughter looked ashamed.

The leader called me over and slapped me hard across the face.

"Why did you take her money?" he asked.

"Were you there when I took anything from her? How could you believe her without proof?" I gathered my courage and stood my ground.

Luck was on my side. The leader paused, then said, "It's none of my business who owes whom. You'll pay your own share," he told the old woman.

Then he turned and left.

That day, many of the captives made their phone calls. The system here was no different than the desert. For those like me who couldn't pay or call anyone, the threat remained: "Your lives will be hell."

Those words echoed in my mind every day.

After the guards left, I went to the old woman.

"Why did you lie?" I asked.

She insisted I had taken her money. When I realized she wouldn't back down, I walked away.

To my surprise, her daughter approached me a few minutes later and quietly apologized for her mother's behavior.

She was gentle and polite—a kind soul in a cruel place.

From that day onward, our routine never changed.

We were herded into the courtyard for meals.

Afterward, those who hadn't paid were lined up against the wall. One by one, they were dragged forward—beaten, their heads slammed against the concrete, their backs whipped with metal rods and chains.

Waiting for your turn was worse than the beating itself. I could feel the pain even before it began.

Blood stained the ground.

Broken ribs, fractured limbs—it became normal.

No one came to help.

No one heard our screams.

I refused to cry or groan. I had seen how they beat harder when people screamed. I wanted to survive, and I couldn't afford any injuries—especially not now. I still had one dream left: to one-day play football again. And that dream, somehow, gave me the strength to endure.

In the prison of Sabha, Libya, I lost my sense of time. I didn't know the date or how long I'd been there. Days and nights blended into a blur of pain and fear. I believe it was more than a week when the thought of escape first took root in my mind.

Every day, when they herded us into the courtyard, I'd hear other prisoners whispering about escape. The girls, in particular, encouraged us.

Why don't you try to escape?" a Somalian girl asked me one day.

She had brought me a few sweets, a gesture of kindness in a place void of it. Her face was mostly covered, but I could see the sharpness and strength in her eyes.

We never saw them torture the girls. I assumed they had other plans for them—maybe worse.

"How could we do that?" I asked, genuinely baffled.

"Simple," she said, tilting her head slightly toward the compound wall. "Just jump over that wall and run."

At first, I thought she was joking. But when I followed her gaze and studied the wall, I realized she might be right.

It wasn't impossible.

"It's better to die than endure all this pain and humiliation," she said quietly, then walked away.

That anonymous Somalian girl had shown me the way out.

From that moment, every time I looked at that wall, I no longer saw a barrier—I saw a chance.

It was high, sure, and I knew it wouldn't be easy. But it was there.

It existed.

And that was enough.

In situations like this, I always thought of Ahmed—my friend, my brother in everything but blood. We planned things together, encouraged each other, pushed one another to the edge. Being with him gave me strength. But now, he was gone. Killed. And I was alone.

That wall reminded me once again that Ahmed would never be there for me again.

Then, one night, the chance came.

We had gathered in the courtyard as usual, waiting for the evening meal.

The air was heavy with silence and fatigue.

As they started serving the food, a girl suddenly broke from the group and ran toward the compound wall.

She stood there, hands cupped together like a cradle, and shouted loudly in Somali.

"Run! Run!"

I understood instantly.

She was offering herself as a step.

I ran toward her.

It was the same girl who had given me sweets. Brave, fearless, defiant. I placed one foot into her hands, the other on her shoulder. In a swift movement, I scrambled to the top of the wall.

My heart was pounding as I jumped to the other side and hit the ground running.

Out of hundreds of prisoners, only ten of us escaped that night.

We scattered into the darkness, running blindly through the streets of the city.

We didn't know where we were going—only that we had to keep moving.

Behind us, the prison erupted.

Dogs barked.

Engines roared to life.

Gunshots rang through the air.

I could feel bullets slicing past me.

When I turned a corner, I looked back and saw one of the escapees had been hit by a car.

He died instantly.

Eventually, they caught us—every last one of us.

They brought us back to the prison, bloodied and broken.

That night, they tortured us until they were exhausted.

My entire body ached.

But I was still alive.

I hadn't suffered a fatal blow, nor had they crippled me.

Lying there, my back against the cold wall of the room, I promised myself something:

This wasn't over.

I would escape again.

Life soon returned to our daily abnormal routine.

The escape attempt had changed things—now, they never left us unguarded in the courtyard.

Armed men stood watch near the compound wall whenever we were brought out for meals or punishment. Two guards, always, rifles in hand.

But I had noticed something from the window of our cell: once we were locked inside, the courtyard was unguarded.

That window became my new obsession.

Fitted with thick vertical iron bars, it looked impossible.

Still, I stared at it every day, the way I used to stare at the compound wall.

If there was to be another escape, it would have to be through that window—at night.

We began discussing ideas.

Someone suggested breaking the bars, but we quickly dismissed it.

We didn't have tools, and the risk of being heard was too great.

That plan would get us killed.

Still, I kept looking at the window, willing it to become something else—an open door, a hole in the wall, a way out.

I even started to hallucinate.

In my mind, the bars faded.

I could almost see myself passing through.

Then, one afternoon as we sat together in the room, someone said,

"I think I can slide through those bars."

"Not possible," another prisoner replied. "They're too narrow. You'll get stuck."

To prove his point, the first man got up and tried.

He squeezed himself halfway in but couldn't move any further.

His body jammed between the cold iron rods.

We all jumped to our feet, watching anxiously.

As I looked at him struggle, a memory from my childhood flashed in my mind.

Back in Kismayo, we played a game where we'd try to squeeze through narrow iron gates.

We'd rub oil on our bodies to help us slip through.

It worked.

"We can do it," I said, my mind racing. "If we make our bodies slippery enough, we can slide through."

"What can we use?" someone asked.

"We don't have oil," I said, "but what about soap?"

It was the best idea we had.

Everyone agreed.

The next day was our shower day.

We planned carefully.

Each of us saved the soap they gave us and hoarded some water from mealtime.

That day, many didn't bathe properly or drink much—we were saving every drop and every sliver of soap for our escape.

After breakfast, we returned to our cell with our water and waited for the guards to lock us in for the day.

It was late afternoon when the last door clanged shut and the guards walked away from the compound wall.

This was our moment to test the plan.

We gathered near the window.

A few of us kept watch at the door.

One man stripped down, lathered his body with the soap and water we had saved, and approached the bars.

We watched with bated breath.

He squeezed through slowly, grimacing with pain. The pressure of the metal was intense, but the soap did its job.

He made it.

He was on the other side.

We nearly cheered—but held it in.

It was still daylight.

There was no way we could escape now without being seen. So, reluctantly, painfully, he slid back inside.

But the test had worked.

It was possible.

We had a way out.

That night, we would try again—for real.

I could barely contain my excitement.

For the first time in days, hope felt real again.

After dinner, we waited.

Hours passed.

We said little, each of us lost in our thoughts, our fear, our fragile hope.

My heart was pounding so hard I could feel it in my throat. I knew that if they caught us this time, there would be no mercy.

They'd kill us.

Around midnight, we began.

The first man removed his clothes, threw them through the window, and rubbed his body down with soap and water.

Image Credits: AI generated image by Malick Mahmood

One man stripped down, lathered his body with the soap, & approached the bars. He squeezed through slow, grimacing with pain. The pressure of the metal was intense, but the soap did its job. He made it. He was on the other side.

Silently, slowly, he slid between the iron bars and disappeared into the night.

One by one, more followed.

Within minutes, ten of us were outside.

The compound wall was only a few yards away, but the danger wasn't over.

Some of our captors were sleeping in the courtyard.

We crouched low and moved slowly, like shadows. Every step felt like it might be our last.

One of us took position near the wall, forming a foothold with his clasped hands.

One by one, we climbed up and over.

I saw a few more men slide through the window behind me before I jumped down on the other side of the wall.

We had agreed not to run together. That would make us easy to catch. Instead, we split into smaller groups and scattered in different directions into the dark streets of Sabha.

Getting out of the prison turned out to be the easy part.

What came next was worse.

Almost every other house in the surrounding neighborhood belonged to a gang of human traffickers. We didn't know which way to go. Every step outside that prison felt like we were running straight into another trap.

As we moved through the darkness, I saw armed men lurking near alleyways.

Suddenly, someone shouted from behind us: "Stop or we shoot!"

We froze.

We had no choice.

We knew they wouldn't hesitate.

In Libya, they didn't shoot to wound—they shot to kill. If we ran, they might use us for target practice.

We had walked into the hands of another gang of Libyan bandits.

New torture was different and more calculated. Every day after breakfast, they forced us to stand outside in the blistering sun. We stood for hours, our bodies slowly cooking under the relentless heat.

They hit us, slapped us, cursed us.

We were herded like cattle, shoved down streets until we reached another large house—another prison.

This one was worse.

It was bigger than the last, with hundreds of other prisoners crammed inside.

The guards here were more disciplined, the compound more secure. Everything about this place said: you're not getting out.

I looked around and thought, these Libyans are more organized than the others.

And I knew, deep down, I was about to face another round of torture. But pain wasn't new to me. I had carried it with me since we left Ethiopia. It had become part of me—an expectation, almost a companion.

Freedom, on the other hand, still felt like a dream that kept slipping further away.

To my surprise, they didn't beat us or demand money this time. But the new torture was different—and more calculated.

Every day after breakfast, they forced us to stand outside in the blistering sun.

We stood for hours, our bodies slowly cooking under the relentless heat.

One by one, people collapsed.

Some fainted, others convulsed.

When someone dropped, a stretcher would arrive and carry them away.

No one ever came back.

We never knew what happened to them—whether they were alive or dead.

They simply vanished.

I stayed in that second prison for several weeks. The routine never changed. Stand in the sun, survive the heat, collapse and disappear—or make it to nightfall and be locked in a giant, suffocating room. Some slept, their bodies giving in to exhaustion.

I couldn't.

My mind was too haunted, too afraid.

One night, while most were asleep, I heard a voice whisper from the dark: "I don't understand why they never bring back the sick after giving them treatment."

Another voice, deeper and closer to the corner of the room, replied, calm and matter-of-fact: "Because they're not treating them. They're cutting them open... for their organs."

The room fell still.

He told us he had once been among the sick. He collapsed under the sun and woke in a makeshift operation theatre.

What he saw when he opened his eyes would never leave him: doctors, real doctors, cutting open a refugee on the next table, harvesting his organs.

"No matter what," he warned, "don't fall. Don't complain about anything. If you do, you'll never come back."

He went silent.

I don't know how many others were awake to hear that, but I was. And from that moment on, I was petrified.

Every day under that burning sun, my only goal was simple: stay standing. Survive.

Then, one night, everything changed.

We had just been let out into the compound for dinner when gunfire erupted at the front gate.

An attack.

Another group had come to raid the prison.

The guards who had been watching us rushed to the front lines, leaving the compound momentarily exposed.

"Run! Run!" someone screamed, and in an instant, the entire compound erupted into chaos.

Prisoners bolted toward the wall.

I ran too, my legs moving on instinct.

Bullets started flying.

One of the guards spotted us and opened fire. Men around me were hit. They screamed, fell, died.

I kept running.

As I climbed the wall, the man next to me was shot.

As he fell backward, he grabbed my ankle, yanking me down with him.

"Please… help me. I don't want to die," he begged, his eyes wide with fear.

I looked down at him, my heart breaking—but I couldn't stop. I couldn't save him. I wasn't strong enough to carry him. I had to pry his fingers off my leg, and then I kicked free.

Between bursts of gunfire, I scrambled over the wall and vanished into the night.

This time, I wasn't alone.

Four of us ran together, blind to where we were going—only that we had to get away.

After two hours of silent running, we found a house in ruins and crept inside.

We said nothing.

Even whispering felt too risky.

We just huddled in silence, waiting for dawn.

When the sun rose, we spotted a taxi cab parked a short distance away. It was our only chance.

We debated what to do.

We had no money.

No plan.

But we decided to talk to the driver anyway and try to get him to take us to Tripoli.

One of the others came with me.

I approached the driver and asked him if he could take us to the port city.

He eyed us suspiciously but agreed—so long as we promised to pay whatever amount he asked once we arrived.

We climbed in.

The whole ride, we were tense, afraid he might sell us to another gang. But he didn't. He just drove.

About thirty minutes in, exhaustion overtook me.

I fell asleep.

When I woke up, we were in Tripoli.

The chaos of the city—the honking, shouting, buzzing of life—jolted me awake.

The driver told us we were close to our destination.

He seemed to believe that we were visiting family.

Eventually, he pulled up in front of a house and said, "This is it."

We told him to wait while we went inside to get the money. He demanded that one of us stay behind as collateral.

We smiled, lied, and reassured him.

Then all four of us got out.

We walked into what looked like an empty house… and slipped out the back.

From our new hiding spot, we watched as the taxi driver waited. He stood outside his cab, then approached the house. But when no one answered, he returned to his car—angry, but defeated—and eventually drove away.

We waited until late afternoon before stepping out.

The streets of Tripoli were foreign and cold.

We had no contacts, no money, no plan. All we could do was search for someone—anyone—who might help.

We wandered aimlessly, hoping to stumble upon a friendly face. We saw a few Somalis and tried talking to them, but they were just like us—lost, desperate, and looking for someone to help.

We eventually found help.

A tall Somalian took us to an unfinished building packed with dirty mattresses—some already occupied.

He pointed out a few vacant spots. "Keep your shoes on and your belongings under your head," he warned. "Local authorities and militiamen patrol these places. If they catch you, you're dead."

My companions collapsed onto the mattresses and fell asleep.

I couldn't rest.

Instead, I stepped outside with our Somalian guide.

We talked about my predicament.

"Everybody on the street claims they can help you cross the Mediterranean," he said. "Most will steal your money and vanish."

"So how do I get out of here?" I asked.

"I know some well-connected Somali smugglers. I'll introduce you," he replied.

Relief flooded me.

I begged him to take me to them.

He agreed, and we set off.

On the way, we traded stories. "I once tried to cross from Libya to Italy," he said. "Our boat of a hundred caught fire and sank a kilometer offshore. Most drowned—they couldn't swim. I couldn't either, but a stranger held me up and gave me an empty oil canister to float on. He saved me… and drowned himself."

Tears glistened in his eyes. "God works in mysterious ways," he murmured.

Since then, he'd dedicated himself to helping refugees.

"Will you ever leave Tripoli?" I asked.

"Once money arrives from home, yes," he said.

As we walked down a busy street, he suddenly stopped.

Across the road, a Libyan was signaling for us to come over.

We complied, hoping not to arouse suspicion.

Instead, he handed me a broom. "Clean in front of my restaurant," he snarled.

I wanted to strike him, but I swept the pavement instead.

He fetched another broom, handed it to my companion, then deliberately scattered fresh garbage where we had just worked.

No water, no gratitude—just contempt.

I realized then how little these people saw us as human.

Libya was a hub for every kind of trafficking—including the export of human organs.

We said nothing and continued to our meeting.

By Maghreb, we reached a locked house with a heavy padlock.

My Somalian friend knocked; someone peered through the crack and spoke briefly, then told us to return after dark.

We retreated to a crowded street. "If you want to go back, go," I told him. "I'm staying."

After a moment's thought, he decided to wait with me—he was the first honest man I'd met since Kismayo.

We hung around until night fell.

Returning to the locked door, we knocked again.

A different Somali voice called us in.

We followed him down narrow alleys until we reached a small office-like house.

Inside, we sat and waited.

An hour later, he returned with another Somalian man.

The newcomer looked me over and asked, "You want Italy?"

At my nod, he quoted $800 per person for the boat trip. I shook my head. "I have no money, but I know GPS navigation."

They hesitated—until they realized I was serious.

Then they said, "We need a GPS operator for the next boat. It leaves in two days. You go free."

I exhaled. "Free?"

"Yes."

We left after arranging details: where to meet, when, what to bring.

My Somali companion promised to get me there on time.

Walking back to our hiding place, I was terrified of Libyan patrols—but God guided us safely home.

That night, sleep was impossible. My mind raced with memories of home, the tortures endured, and the anxiety of what lay ahead.

After Fajr prayer the next morning, my companion and I walked two hours to the meeting point.

When we arrived, they refused to let him inside—only those on the travel list were allowed.

We hugged, promised to reunite safely in Europe, and I walked in alone.

Inside a cramped office waited about ten people—refugees. I was the only one who hadn't paid.

By noon, they herded us into a jeep.

As we rumbled away from the city, I feared they would abandon us back to the desert. Only the rising scent of salt air reassured me: we were still heading toward the sea.

Three hours later, we reached a farmhouse.

Sixty or seventy people, including visibly pregnant women, crowded the yard.

We waited there until almost midnight, when a medium-sized flatbed truck appeared.

Eighty or ninety of us climbed onto its crowded back.

After two more hours of jarring travel, the driver stopped us near a cluster of scrubby trees.

We stumbled off.

Two armed men emerged from the woods and marched us deeper into the bush—into a large metal cage.

They locked the gate.

We were packed in like livestock.

For two days and nights, we remained sealed inside with no food and only a foul-smelling, contaminated water pipe. We drank it anyway.

Four pregnant women groaned in agony, but no one came to help.

We were invisible, disposable—our lives had no value here.

One night, between prayers, I spoke with one of the pregnant women, who writhed in pain.

"Why did you get pregnant on this journey? Where is your husband?" I asked gently.

She looked at me with haunted eyes and said simply, "I was raped."

I had no words.

The stench grew worse each hour.

No one could sleep.

It became impossible to find a clean spot even to pray.

On the second night, after Isha, three men arrived—two guards who shoved a stranger into the cage.

"He is your boat driver," one guard announced mockingly, "so treat him respectfully."

We clustered around the man, peppering him with questions: How long to Italy? When do we leave? He said nothing—only asked desperately for water.

He drank deeply from that vile pipe.

Finally, he spoke: "Who is the GPS operator?"

My heart pounded.

I hesitated—fearful it might endanger me further—then raised my hand.

"That would be me," I said, stepping forward.

He nodded, but offered no reassurance.

Around us, refugees whispered: did any of us really have a chance?

That night, the guards returned and unlocked the cage.

"Follow us," they barked.

We trailed them for three hours through the dark. At dawn, we arrived at a deserted beach. A small, battered boat bobbed in the surf.

Three tall Libyan smugglers waited. They shouted at us to hurry into line.

Our boat driver turned to me, alarmed. "This boat can't handle eighty or ninety people!" he warned.

Before anyone could answer, the ringleader strode forward and demanded, "Who is the GPS operator?"

I stepped up and answered.

He produced the GPS unit, firelight glinting off its screen, and quizzed me on its settings and coordinates.

When I asked, "Can you switch it to English?" the smugglers laughed.

"An Englishman going to an English country!" one mocked.

They finally relented, and the ringleader declared us ready to depart.

But our driver wasn't convinced.

He pointed at the flimsy vessel. "You expect me to load this with so many people?"

The leader sneered. "We've used this boat many times—no problem. Besides, you have an English GPS operator now." He slapped me on the cheek with filthy hands.

The driver refused, and the argument grew heated.

I wanted to intervene, but I was too afraid.

Then, in a flash, the leader drew a pistol and shot the driver in the head.

I saw the bullet pierce his forehead.

He collapsed, brains spilling out the back of his skull. The leader fired two more warning shots into the night air.

Across the Mediterranean

"All of you get into that boat or we'll start shooting you," the leader announced.

We had no choice but to run toward the boat.

As we ran, the smugglers began throwing rocks at us. Something heavy struck me behind my right ear.

I instantly felt dizzy.

I would have fallen, but someone held me and dragged me to the boat.

I'm sure that if I hadn't been their GPS operator, they would have left me there to die. They needed me, so they had to help me on board.

The last thing I remember after getting into the boat was vomiting. I hadn't eaten in two days and there was nothing in my stomach, so it felt like my insides were being ripped out.

I heard the boat's engine roar to life—and then I passed out. Who was driving the boat? I had no idea.

When I woke up, it was dark. I remembered seeing the sunrise before we left, so I realized I'd been unconscious all day. My head was still spinning. I couldn't even hold it upright.

Then someone said, "The GPS operator is back!" and in no time they brought the device to me. But I couldn't focus on the screen. I was still nauseous and felt like vomiting again.

Almost crawling, I made my way to the front of the boat. I leaned over and threw up again—just a small amount of green fluid this time.

I felt like even my arteries were going to come out. I was so weak, I passed out again.

Image Credits: AI generated image by Malick Mahmood

The boat was made of plastic, filled with air like a giant bag. It looked like it could sink with a single puncture. It was simply floating, waves rocking it gently from side to side.

The next day, I came to my senses when I felt the sunlight on my face. I opened my eyes and looked around.

A woman was sitting near me with a baby in her lap. Others sat on makeshift wooden bench-type seats. The boat was made of plastic, filled with air like a giant bag. It looked like it could sink with a single puncture.

I thought about the fact that I didn't even know how to swim.

I tried to sit up, but my head was still spinning.

I no longer cared whether I lived or died.

As my eyes adjusted to the brightness of the sun, I looked at the woman with the baby and asked, "Who's driving the boat?" I asked because I couldn't hear the sound of an engine.

She told me someone else was driving it. "It's been almost two days since we left," she added.

Although I was too weak to stand, my mind was beginning to work.

I knew something was wrong.

The journey from Tripoli to Italy was supposed to be only eight to ten hours.

We'd clearly been lost.

I asked her why the engine was silent.

She replied, "The driver turned it off. We ran out of fuel."

What I saw—and what I heard—gave me no hope.

No strength.

I passed out again.

The next morning, two people helped me sit upright.

It was our third day in the Mediterranean.

Our boat was simply floating, waves rocking it gently from side to side.

Someone handed me the GPS again. When I looked at it, I couldn't understand anything—it had been reset to a language I didn't recognize.

On the fifth day, around noon, someone shouted the words we'd been longing to hear: "There's a ship there!"
Everyone instantly turned toward where he was pointing. Far on the horizon, I could see it.

Image Credits: AI generated image by Malick Mahmood

Someone had fiddled with it.

I spent over an hour restoring the settings and finally got it back to English. When I could finally read the display, I saw we were 80 kilometers from Malta.

"We're 80 kilometers from Malta!" I announced.

"We only have about half a gallon of fuel left," the person driving the boat said loudly. "We're saving it in case we see a ship or boat nearby."

"So there's nothing we can do except wait," I said quietly.

The others nodded in agreement.

Life in the boat was much like life in the desert. The only difference was the surroundings—blue water instead of sand. But the hunger, thirst, the scorching sun during the day, and the freezing wind at night—they were all the same. In some ways, the boat was worse. We couldn't even move around to stretch our legs. We had to stay in our spots. And even standing was risky: if one person stood, someone on the other side had to stand too, to keep the balance and avoid capsizing.

On the fifth day, around noon, someone shouted the words we'd been longing to hear: "There's a ship there!"

Everyone instantly turned toward where he was pointing.

Far on the horizon, I could see it.

The driver quickly started the engine and we sped toward the ship.

Just when I feared they might not have seen us, the ship began turning in our direction—and blew its horn.

"Throw away the GPS!" someone shouted from behind. I didn't hesitate. I threw it into the sea.

The ship completed its turn and began motoring straight toward us.

"They're coming! We're safe!" Many people started clapping and cheering.

It was a fishing trawler.

From its deck, someone announced over a microphone that they were from Italy. Everyone turned to look at me—I was the only one who could speak English.

Two men helped me stand.

I could barely keep my balance.

I shouted toward the Italian trawler, telling them we were refugees and in very bad condition. I explained that we had been lost for days, that many among us were sick, hungry, and thirsty. I told them there were four pregnant women on board.

They responded that they had contacted the Malta Marines and help would arrive soon.

The Italian ship didn't take us on board, but they stayed close. They threw over water bottles, food packs, and even white cotton sheets to help shield us from the sun.

Suddenly, one of the pregnant women began to scream in pain. The others shouted that she was about to give birth. We held the sheets around her while the other women helped.

Someone asked me to request scissors from the captain to cut the baby's umbilical cord.

"Has she already delivered the baby?" the captain asked.

"Not yet," I replied.

"Then wait a few more minutes. Help is almost there," he said.

It was then that another, much larger ship appeared from behind the fishing trawler.

A military ship.

The Malta Marines had arrived. They anchored a short distance away, then we saw small boats dropping into the sea from the back of the ship. One of them approached us. Soldiers stood inside, some holding automatic weapons, aimed at us.

"We are coming near you to help and we don't want any trouble," one of them said over a loudspeaker. "We are

Malta Marines, and we acknowledge your international human rights."

That was the first time I had ever heard the words human rights in my entire life.

The soldiers on the boat helped the pregnant woman climb aboard.

Before heading back to their ship, they told us they'd return soon to get the rest of us. We watched as they took her to their military vessel.

Not long after, a helicopter appeared in the sky and hovered above the ship.

We saw them lower a stretcher, gently place the woman on it, and then lift her into the helicopter.

As I watched her ascend into the sky, I whispered a prayer from my heart for her and those who were helping her: "May God be with you."

We waited there for another two hours before another boat, again carrying Malta Marines, arrived.

They told us we were going to be transferred to an Italian Navy ship, and that it would be up to the Italians to decide what happened next.

But there was a problem—they weren't going to take us onboard. Instead, we had to follow them in our own boat.

"How can we follow you? Our engine is broken," our boat driver said.

I knew he must have done something to the engine on purpose, hoping the Malta Marines would take us onboard instead.

We didn't want to remain in that fragile, overloaded plastic boat any longer. But our plan didn't work.

The Marines sent one of their engineers to check the engine. He brought a toolbox and fixed it within minutes.

They gave us some fuel, life jackets, and one large flashlight. "Follow us closely," they instructed. "If you need help for any reason, flash this light on and off."

Late in the afternoon, we started following the Malta Marine ship.

As darkness fell, we kept our eyes on its many lights to stay on course. We had no light of our own—only the flashlight, which we were told to use only in an emergency.

That night was brutally cold.

Waves crashed into the boat, soaking us to the bone.

We were cold, wet, and shivering, but we had no choice but to keep going.

We followed them for many hours before a massive ship appeared on the horizon.

As it drew closer, I saw that it was an Italian Navy vessel.

The Malta Marine ship stopped.

A smaller boat came over from it and told us that from now on, we would be under the care of the Italian Navy.

The Malta Marines left, and we slowly motored toward the Italian ship.

A rope ladder was thrown down for us to climb.

Those too weak to climb were helped by crew members; a few were lifted up in stretchers.

It was nearly Asr time by the time we were all safely onboard.

They gave us water, juice, milk, and food.

Then they washed us down with hoses—cold water sprayed on us from above while we still had our clothes on. Maybe it was to clean us. Maybe just to cool us down.

"Can anyone speak English?" one of the Italian officers asked.

The refugees pointed at me.

I stepped forward and said, "Yes, I can." And just like that, I became the interpreter for the group.

One of the Italian personnel explained that we were now aboard an Italian Navy ship headed toward the port of Sicily. Once there, we would be dealt with by Italian immigration authorities in accordance with international human rights and refugee laws.

As he spoke, the ship's whistle blew, and we began to move. The sun was just beginning to set.

I looked out over the water, my thoughts drifting to my friend Ahmed and his painful death.

I couldn't hold back the tears.

Who could have imagined, when we left Kismayo together, that he would never make it to the peaceful lands of Europe?

Only twenty minutes later, the ship's whistle blew again.

Sicily appeared on the horizon.

People on the deck began crying with joy, hugging one another. I stood up too, and without any particular reason, I raised my hand and started waving toward the land.

As we entered the harbor, I saw a crowd gathered at the docks.

There were ambulances with flashing lights—nothing like the ones I had seen back in Kismayo. These were modern, clean, fully equipped.

I saw journalists with cameras, news crews, and dozens of vehicles marked UNHCR—United Nations High Commission for Refugees.

My entire journey flashed before my eyes—every hardship, every horror, every loss.

I thought about those who didn't survive. And I thanked God for letting me live to see this day.

As the ship finally came to a stop, I knew I had reached a land where I had human rights—but my journey wasn't over yet.

My destination wasn't Italy. It was Germany.

The ship's whistle blew again, Sicily appeared on the horizon. People began crying in joy, hugging one another. I stood up too, and without any particular reason, I raised my hand and started waving toward the land.

Italy to Munich, Germany

As we anchored at the port of Syracuse, Sicily, a camera crew stood on the dock, photographing our ship.

We were instructed by the authorities to gather near the main exit where a desk had been set up.

Each of us was issued a card with a serial number, and then photographed while holding it.

Afterward, we were led down the stairs to the dockyard.

The moment I stepped onto European soil, I felt a surge of positive energy rise through my body.

For the first time in my life, I felt peace and safety.

Because I could speak English, the Italian authorities asked me to serve as their interpreter.

Representatives from the Italian Red Cross, UNHCR (United Nations High Commission for Refugees), and the International Organization for Migration (IOM) surrounded us, eager to understand our needs.

Although media personnel weren't allowed close, they continued to photograph us from afar.

An immigration officer handed me a clipboard and asked for help collecting the names, birth dates, and nationalities of each refugee.

With the refugees lined up, it was a manageable task.

An officer remained beside me, though sometimes he had to attend to other duties, leaving me to continue alone.

I was aware that we were being registered under the Dublin Regulation, meaning that since we had entered Europe through Italy, we would be required to apply for asylum there.

But my destination was Germany.

I knew Italy had saved us—they rescued us from the sea, fed us, and cared for our sick. I would remain grateful. But

Italy lacked the policies I needed to rebuild: education opportunities and access to sports. Germany offered both.

After we collected the names, the officer instructed me to guide refugees to a row of outdoor stations for fingerprinting.

He explained the Dublin Regulation to me, reiterating that once fingerprinted, a refugee could not legally move to another European country. Attempts to do so would result in being returned to Italy.

While I was registering names, some women were escorted to ambulances. The officer signaled me to go and record their details before they departed. Three were pregnant.

I did as authorities had instructed.

Then I noticed a young Somali man in pain, unable to urinate. The medics were rushing.

As I leaned in to record his details, he pleaded with me: "Don't write my name. I want to go to Germany. I nearly died for it, brother—help me." He gripped my hand tightly.

The medics assumed I had already registered him. They shut the ambulance doors and sped away.

I stood motionless as the ambulance vanished around a corner.

His desperation sparked an idea in me: what if I, too, did not register my name?

Just then, our boat driver appeared and asked, "Is there a way I can avoid being fingerprinted?"

"We owe you, brother," I said.

I began to write his name down as if he had already been taken to the hospital.

He hesitated but eventually thanked me.

I told him that when his name was called, I'd inform the officers he'd already left.

I listed the rest of the refugees and placed my own name at the end.

We were to be transported to a refugee camp once processing finished. "You'll be taken care of at the center," a Red Cross official told me. But I felt dizzy with fatigue, having gone over a week without proper rest or food.

I needed sleep.

As names were called for fingerprinting, I remained alert. When mine was called, it signaled the process was nearly over. My fingerprinting and medical exam took about thirty minutes.

I asked an officer, "Are we done here?"

"Everyone has been processed—except for three," he replied, pointing at names circled in red.

One of them was our boat driver.

"He's the one taken to the hospital," I said.

The officer spoke to a colleague in Italian and then marked the name off.

"What about these two?" he asked.

"I'll look for them," I replied.

Despite my exhaustion, I searched for the missing men.

Almost an hour passed.

Resting briefly on a patch of grass, I overheard some women arguing.

I approached.

Because I had served as the interpreter, many refugees viewed me as a kind of official.

One Somali woman said, "We know who the missing men are," and pointed them out.

I could have informed the authorities, but I approached the men instead.

I warned them that evading fingerprinting might not just risk their future, but could delay everyone's progress.

They agreed to come forward.

By midnight, all fingerprinting was complete. We boarded buses bound for the refugee center.

Only our boat driver had successfully avoided being registered.

The moment I sat in the bus seat, I fell asleep.

We traveled for over thirty minutes before stopping. We were led into a dimly lit hall with mattresses scattered across the floor.

"Welcome to your new home," said one of the officers.

He pointed out bathrooms and assured us the administration would help with any problems.

That night, in Italy, I finally slept deeply and peacefully.

Late the next morning, they gave us breakfast—dry bread and tea.

The clothes I was wearing were filthy, itchy, and stiff with dried sea salt. I desperately wanted to wash them, but I didn't have anything else to wear.

I asked a few of the other men if they had spare clothes. One of them kindly gave me a pair of shorts, which I wore while I washed my clothes.

Once they were clean, I returned the shorts to their owner.

Lunch was spaghetti with a raw tomato placed on top. The spaghetti was undercooked, and the tomato hadn't even been sliced. They handed us two water bottles each and told us we'd need to make them last until dinner. But I had survived the desert—I was already a master at rationing water.

I spent nearly two weeks in that camp and, during that time, developed a stomach disorder from the consistently undercooked food.

I wasn't alone—many others were also falling ill.

One day, a group from the Red Cross visited and asked questions about the food and other facilities. Almost every refugee voiced complaints about the meals. The Red Cross workers said they would look into it, and then they left.

Nothing changed.

During those two weeks, I learned that we had to wait until the Italian immigration office called us individually to process our asylum cases.

The entire situation felt hopeless.

Some refugees had already been waiting for months.

I knew I could escape if I wanted, but I didn't have any money—and I hadn't even called my mother yet.

Within a few days, hundreds of refugees managed to leave the camp. I was still considering my options when two well-dressed men approached me.

They were looking for someone who could speak English to help them get to Germany. They needed someone who could ask for directions, arrange train tickets, find food—whatever was required along the way.

"We can't even ask for directions," one of them said.

"Will you pay me for that?" I asked.

They confirmed they would.

Not only would they cover all my travel expenses to Germany, but they would also pay me $100 upfront for my help.

After we struck the deal, one of them went off to find us good food. I used that time to buy a cheap second-hand phone to call my mom and Ayesha's father.

First I tried Ayesha's father, but the number she had given me didn't work. I tried several times and then gave up.

Then it was time to call Mom.

"Hello? Hello? Is it you, Yousuf?" she said.

Her voice trembled.

I couldn't speak at first. I finally managed to say, "Mom, I'm alive."

That was all she needed to hear.

She burst into prayers and blessings.

I felt a flood of happiness.

I told her I was in Italy and heading to Germany.

The train rolled slowly onto the lower deck of a massive ship.. When we reached the mainland, it simply rolled off and continued its journey. The entire process—was a masterpiece of Italian engineering.

Image Credits: AI generated image by Malick Mahmood

I didn't mention Ahmed's death—I didn't want to worry her yet. I would tell her once I reached Germany.

By the time I hung up, evening had set in.

My new companion returned with fruits and other fresh food. The three of us sat together and ate well.

After that, we began asking around about the fastest and cheapest way to get to Germany.

Everyone agreed: the best option was by train.

We got directions to the train station and left the refugee center later that night.

Everything at the station seemed surprisingly easy.

I just had to buy three adult tickets to Munich, Germany.

As we passed through an automatic door, one of my companions turned to me and smiled. "My mother's prayers are coming true," he said.

"How can you tell?" I asked.

"She always said, one day, doors to your future will open automatically before you." He pointed to the sliding doors. "Didn't you see? The door opened all by itself for me." We all laughed quietly.

Despite everything we had endured, hope was returning. We were finally on our way.

We were in Syracuse, on the Ionian coast of Sicily. From there, trains bound for mainland Italy are ferried across the sea.

It was incredible to witness.

The train rolled slowly onto the lower deck of a massive ship, like a beast boarding a floating fortress. When we reached the mainland, it simply rolled off and continued its journey.

The entire process—a train entering and exiting a ship—was a masterpiece of Italian engineering.

None of us had seen anything like it before.

The train journey stretched on for hours, covering kilometers upon kilometers. With every passing town, I started to feel as if I was almost there—almost at the end of my long, brutal journey. Munich felt closer than ever.

It was late afternoon when we crossed into Austria.

"After Austria, we enter Germany," one of my companions said with quiet excitement.

But then I noticed two uniformed officers walking down the aisle of the train. I assumed they were border police. They were stopping at each seat, asking passengers for travel documents.

When they reached us, they asked to see our passports. We only had train tickets, which we handed to them.

"Passport! Passport!" they kept repeating.

I tried my best to explain that we were refugees on our way to Germany. But they didn't want explanations.

"You three will have to come with us," one of them said firmly.

The train came to a stop at the first Austrian station, and the officers escorted us off.

Other passengers watched us with silent, knowing eyes.

We were taken to a police station, just a 20-minute drive away, in the Austrian border city of Innsbruck.

At the station, a higher-ranking officer spoke to us.

"We're not stopping you from going to Germany or anywhere else," he said, "but you can't enter Austria without the required documents."

He made a few phone calls and then informed us that they would be putting us on a train back to Italy.

We waited for hours in the police station before being escorted back to the railway station sometime after dark.

A train bound for Italy arrived shortly after we did, and the officers placed us aboard.

Not long after the train departed, a ticket collector approached us.

I showed her the tickets we had bought earlier that day for our journey from Syracuse to Munich. By that time train had reached some station and come to halt.

She looked at them and shook her head.

"These tickets are not valid for this train, anyways you may get off" she said, signaling towards the exit.

I tried to explain the situation—that the Austrian police had removed us from another train and put us on this one.

"We didn't board this train on our own," I said. "The police made us get on, and these are the tickets we had when—"

She cut me off gently.

"Sir, this is the train's last stop," she said with a polite smile.

I felt my face flush with quiet embarrassment.

She turned and walked away as I stood there, not knowing what to say.

"What did she say?" one of my companions asked.

"She said this is the last stop," I replied.

We stepped off the train in silence.

We were back in Bolzano, Italy—just across the Austrian border.

Not knowing what else to do, we simply began walking away from the train station, uncertain and quiet.

Soon, we noticed a man standing some distance away, motioning for us to come over.

He looked African—perhaps Eritrean.

We felt a flicker of hope.

Maybe he could help.

We approached him eagerly.

It turned out he was a different kind of human trafficker—calmer, more polished—and he offered to help us, for a price.

I immediately feared my companions might abandon me, thinking they had found someone better equipped to get them to Germany.

The man told us he had been in Italy legally for almost a year. "I've helped many refugees cross into Germany," he said.

"And I don't charge much."

"How much per person?" I asked bluntly.

"It depends on your legal status," he replied.

I explained our situation: we had escaped from the refugee camp in Syracuse, and our fingerprints were already in the Italian system.

"We tried taking the train to Germany, but the Austrians turned us back at the border. They wouldn't let us travel without documents."

After learning about our status, the Eritrean man nodded thoughtfully, then said, "For you, it will be €150 each—for documents and photographs."

"Does that include tickets?" one of my companions asked.

He gave a short laugh. "Are you kidding? That's just for the paperwork. Tickets are separate. Do you know how hard it is to arrange these things?"

"But we don't have any money," my companion admitted.

At that, the man's demeanor shifted.

The friendliness dimmed.

He made it clear that without payment, there would be no help.

We stepped aside for a brief discussion.

My companions assured him they could have the money wired, and they convinced him to proceed.

What surprised and relieved me most was that they agreed to pay for me as well.

"We'll pay €450—for all three of us," one of them said.

They also explained we'd need someone with valid identification to receive the money through Western Union.

The Eritrean gave us his details without hesitation.

He was clearly experienced.

He later led us to a street where clusters of refugees were sleeping against buildings and sprawled on sidewalks.

"You can spend the night here," he said casually, pointing toward a patch of cold pavement.

"I'll find you in the morning, and we'll go to the bank together."

As he walked away, one of my companions turned to me and asked,

"Can we trust him? I mean, we're transferring money to his name."

"It's safe," I assured them.

"We'll provide your mobile number to the sender. That way, he can't collect the money without the PIN we receive."

They thought about it for a moment and nodded in agreement.

And just like that, we were left to sleep out on the roadside, surrounded by strangers and streetlight shadows.

The pavement was hard, and the night air bit through our clothes.

It was cold—unforgivingly cold.

One of my companions started feeling sick and his body was burning with fever. I gave him my jacket, and the other man gave him his T-shirt, but he kept shivering.

I told them I was going to look for something we could use to cover ourselves.

As I walked along the road, I saw people sleeping under blankets—some even under cardboard.

I wondered what my future might be like in Italy.

Eventually, I saw a restaurant with tables outside.

It looked like they were getting ready to close for the night.

A waiter was removing the tablecloths. I thought I'd ask for one, but just as I walked toward him, someone called him from inside and he left without the sheets.

By the time he disappeared indoors, I had reached the tables—and without much thought or reasoning, I simply picked up the tablecloths and left.

By the time I got back, the sick man needed more to cover himself.

We put all the sheets on him, but he still shivered through the night. We tried to get under the sheets with him, but they weren't big enough for all three of us.

In spite of the cold, I eventually fell asleep.

There had been a profound change in me since arriving in Europe. I had started to sleep well—even on dirty mattresses or hard surfaces.

For the first time in my life, I felt safe.

I woke up the next morning to the sound of cars driving by. When the sun came out, we finally felt warm and a little better.

Later that morning, we got a message from Western Union on our phone: our money had arrived.

We were waiting for the Eritrean to come so we could collect it. We had no money and hadn't eaten anything the day before.

"As soon as he gets here, we'll go to the nearest Western Union and get our money. Then I'd like us to have a nice lunch," said the man who had been sick the night before. We smiled back at him.

He was certainly right about the lunch.

The Eritrean had promised he'd come early, but it was already afternoon and he still hadn't shown up.

We didn't even have his phone number.

I was about to lose hope when I saw him walking toward us. He told us he'd been delayed by important matters. "We better hurry. Western Union closes soon," he warned.

It was already dark by the time we collected the money and had arranged for our photographs.

We had to spend another night on the footpath because the Eritrean wouldn't hand over our documents until the next day.

He wanted half of his payment then, but we told him we wouldn't pay until we had our papers.

After dropping us off at the same spot we had slept the night before, he left.

Our sick friend had carried the sheets all day, which meant we at least had something for the cold night.

The Eritrean returned early the next day.

He seemed eager to get paid.

He handed us fake documents written in Italian, with our names and photos.

He claimed they would help us travel across Austria.

I wasn't sure—they didn't look like any real documents I had ever seen—but we had no choice, so we took them.

He began demanding his money, but we pushed back, saying the documents weren't good enough.

After a short negotiation, we agreed to pay him €200 for all three of us, but only after he took us to a bus stop where we could catch a ride to Germany.

Someone had told us the road border checks were more relaxed than the train ones, so the bus was a safer option.

All four of us went to the bus station and boarded a bus to Munich.

"You'll be in Munich in six hours," the Eritrean said.

We paid him €200 and he left.

At around four in the morning, I woke up. I was relieved to see the bus still moving—it meant we had crossed the border into Germany. I looked out the window and saw a sign: "Munich 10 km."

Image Credits: AI generated image by Malick Mahmood

The bus was scheduled to depart after dinnertime. After eating and offering our Isha prayers, our bus finally departed from Bolzano.

We were nervous—if this attempt failed, we wouldn't have the money to try again.

There were very few passengers, mostly white people speaking Italian or German.

At around four in the morning, I woke up.

I was relieved to see the bus still moving—it meant we had crossed the border into Germany.

I looked out the window and saw a sign: "Munich 10 km."

Excited, I woke my companions. "*Mabrook* (congratulations) brothers—we're in Germany."

They smiled back.

We were lucky.

No one had asked to see our fake documents.

We arrived in Munich as the city was waking up.

The bus reached Allianz Arena, the famous football stadium. As it made a turn, I quickly decided to get off. I approached the driver and asked to be let out. I hugged my companions, got off, and stepped onto soil of Germany.

I had chosen the stadium as my final destination because football had always been my life—and I believed it would shape my future.

It was early, and only a few people were around.

I saw an African man approaching and asked him for directions to a mosque.

He guided me to one nearby.

After prayers, I spoke with a few men there. They helped me find a refugee camp.

The first thing I did there was call my mother.

I told her I was safe and had made it to Munich.

The bus reached Allianz Arena. As it made a turn, I quickly decided to get off. I had chosen the stadium as my final destination because football had always been my life—and I believed it would shape my future.

We were both happy, but the mood turned somber when I told her about Ahmed. I asked her to visit his family and give them the heartbreaking news. We were still speaking about him when the call dropped—I had run out of credit.

The refugee center in Munich wasn't much different from the one in Syracuse, Italy.

I stayed there for four days.

On the first day, I filed for asylum and was interviewed by a court official. She told me I'd be transferred to a shelter in another city once the court processed my application.

"When can I leave?" I asked.

"Soon after the court issues the certificate directing you to the refugee shelter," she replied, explaining that it could take a day or two.

I would need to come back daily to check.

So, for the next three days, I waited at the court from six in the morning to six in the evening. On Friday, a security officer told us to return on Monday.

Some refugees left, but I stayed.

I wasn't sure what else to do.

I stood near an automatic door that led to the court offices. Only those with a security card could enter. Then I saw a security officer approach and swipe his card. The door opened. Before it locked again, I quickly slipped a piece of paper between the frame and lock. Once the guard walked away, I stepped inside.

Within minutes, I was at the door of the official who had interviewed me.

She was surprised to see me.

I explained that I desperately wanted to leave the refugee center.

She agreed to help.

"How did you get in here?" she asked.

"Madam, I've crossed two continents to get here. Your automatic door wasn't going to stop me," I said.

She smiled slightly, then told me to wait outside.

After almost an hour, I knocked again.

"Oh, you're still here? I'm sorry—I forgot," she said.

She invited me into her office and quickly finished my paperwork. I got my transfer certificate and a letter for the ticket clerk at the train station, who would issue me a ticket to Gezen.

I thanked her and walked to the railway station.

The clerk told me I'd have to wait until 8:00 a.m. to get my ticket.

I had nowhere to go, so I just waited on the platform.

Late at night, two police officers approached and asked for my documents.

I showed them what I had, but they said I needed a temporary ID. They took me to a nearby police station and held me until morning.

Then they issued a temporary paper with my photo and details. "Next time someone asks for ID, show them this," the officer said.

Back at the station, I handed the clerk my letter, and she gave me a train ticket to Gezen, with a transfer in Frankfurt.

While I waited at the platform, two more police officers came and asked for my documents.

I gave them everything, but I was tired and frustrated.

I argued with them, asking why they had picked me out of everyone.

They politely repeated that they were just doing their job.

After they left, I noticed a German girl who sat beside me.

I looked at her.

"Life is not easy out there," she said. "But trust me—we are on your side," and she offered her hand.

Her words were kind, and they calmed me down.

We introduced ourselves. She was on her way to visit her mother and sister in Frankfurt and was studying veterinary science in Munich.

She was beautiful and compassionate. We traveled together to Frankfurt, talking the entire time. She even bought some fruits for us to share.

When we arrived in Frankfurt five hours later, we said goodbye and went our separate ways.

People often ask if my journey has ended.

I tell them: yes, my journey has ended—but it is also the beginning of something else, something I don't yet understand.

I hope one day, I will.

Conclusion

When a person has a story to tell, the hardest part is often knowing where to begin and how to end. Caught in this confusion, many stories are left untold—buried under silence, lost to time. But mine, even if incomplete, has at least found a voice. You've come to know a part of it.

Perhaps even those in high places have heard something of it—that if a person is given life, they deserve the right to live it with dignity. A mother shouldn't live in fear every time her child steps out, uncertain if they will return. Health, education, and safety—these should be basic rights for every human being.

Why do I say this story is incomplete? Because so many chapters remain unwritten—before the beginning and even after the so-called end. So many dimensions of my life are still hidden in the shadows, and worse, there's no mention of those who lie buried beneath the sands of the Sahara or at the bottom of the Mediterranean Sea. No one abandons their home and throws their life into peril unless every door of hope is shut in their own land.

If only Ahmed—my friend—and I had seen even a flicker of hope at home, perhaps we'd still be there, surrounded by our loved ones. But we weren't given that choice.

I often hear Europeans say, "Refugees are taking our jobs and our resources." They have no idea what we've endured just to stand on this soil.

Even before I took my first step, I knew—I knew—there was a 90% chance I would die.

Still, I walked.

"Do you think we're crazy?" I once asked a German girl at the Munich railway station. "Do you think we just prefer

European weather?" She listened to me throughout the five-hour train ride from Munich to Frankfurt.

She kept saying, "I understand you."

I wish I could talk to her again.

I've forgotten her name, though she told it to me.

When we parted ways, I was too embarrassed to ask her to repeat it.

I believe that birth is a lottery.

Some are born into freedom and abundance.

Others into fire and famine. And if the first chance at life leads to a dead end, doesn't everyone deserve the right to seek a second?

For us, migration isn't a choice—it's fire behind and fire ahead. We walk through the flames. I lost a friend along the way. But I survived.

I lived to tell our story.

Today, I am in Ireland, working to earn the highest certification in football coaching. Playing the sport, myself is no longer the same. That realization struck me in Germany, when I got injured while playing for a local club.

During tests and examinations, I discovered that my knees had sustained long-term damage during my journey—damage that can't easily be undone.

As for how and why I moved from Germany to Ireland—that's a story for another time and moreover it is totally a different genre, if I may say so.

In end my only message is this: Let's come together and make this world beautiful—for everyone.

THE END

Glossary of Terms & Phrases

Adhan
The Islamic call to prayer, announced from a mosque five times a day. It serves as a reminder for Muslims to stop and pray, marking the different times of worship throughout the day.

Al-Jihadi
A term used to refer to someone engaged in "jihad." While the word "jihad" literally means "struggle" or "striving" in Arabic, the term "Al-Jihadi" often refers to individuals involved in armed or militant struggle, particularly in extremist or terrorist contexts.

Al-Qaeda
A global militant Islamist organization founded by Osama bin Laden, responsible for numerous terrorist attacks including those on September 11, 2001. The name means "The Base" in Arabic.

Al-Shabab
A militant extremist group based in Somalia, affiliated with Al-Qaeda. They aim to establish an Islamic state in Somalia and have carried out violent attacks both within the country and abroad.

Asr
One of the five daily Islamic prayers. It is performed in the late afternoon, typically midway between noon and sunset.

British-Somaliland
A former British protectorate in the north of present-day Somalia. It existed until 1960, when it merged with Italian Somaliland to form the Republic of Somalia.

Dhuhr
The midday Islamic prayer, performed after the sun passes its zenith and before the Asr prayer.

Fajr
The first of the five daily Islamic prayers, performed at dawn before sunrise. It symbolizes spiritual awakening and discipline.

Haram
An Arabic term meaning "forbidden" in Islam. It can refer to actions, foods, or behaviors that are considered sinful or impermissible under Islamic law.

Hijab
A head covering worn by many Muslim women as a symbol of modesty and privacy. It can also represent cultural identity and religious commitment.

Insha'Allah
A common Arabic phrase meaning "God willing" or "If God wills it." It is often used by Muslims when speaking about future plans or events that are beyond human control.

Isha
The fifth and final daily Islamic prayer, performed at night. It marks the end of the day and brings spiritual closure.

Italian-Somaliland
A former Italian colony in the southern part of present-day Somalia. Along with British Somaliland, it formed the independent state of Somalia in 1960.

Janaza
The Islamic funeral prayer and associated rites. It is a communal obligation for Muslims to pray for the deceased and seek forgiveness for their soul.

Jihad
An Arabic word meaning "struggle" or "effort." In a religious context, it refers to striving in the path of God. This can be spiritual (struggling to live righteously) or, controversially, physical (as in militant struggle), though the latter is often misused and misunderstood.

Mabrook
An Arabic word meaning "Congratulations." Commonly used to express joy at someone's success or good fortune.

Maghreb
One of the five daily prayers in Islam, performed just after sunset.

Qada
This refers to "making up" a missed prayer or fast. If a Muslim misses a required act of worship due to valid reasons, they are expected to perform it later as Qada.

Sahih-Bukhari
One of the most trusted and authoritative collections of Hadith (sayings and actions of the Prophet Muhammad). Compiled by Imam Bukhari, it is highly respected in Islamic scholarship.

Sharia
Islamic law derived from the Quran and Hadith. It governs aspects of both personal and communal life, including rituals, family matters, and legal issues.

Ugali
A traditional East African dish made from maize flour (cornmeal) cooked in boiling water to a dense, dough-like consistency. It is a staple food in Somalia and neighboring countries.

Yallah
An Arabic expression meaning "Let's go" or "Hurry up." It's commonly used in everyday conversation to prompt movement or urgency.

Image Credits: Yousuf Mohammed

About Yousuf Mohammed

Yousuf is the central figure whose journey forms the heart of this book.

Through detailed interviews, he shared his experiences, reflections, and aspirations, bringing his story to life.

Currently pursuing football coaching certifications to reach the highest level in Ireland, Yousuf dreams of one day developing a football academy in Kismayo, aiming to inspire and empower youth through sport.

He firmly believes that social security benefits are not a sustainable solution for refugees—instead, he champions the importance of hard work and self-reliance.

Working as a security officer himself, Yousuf is dedicated to building his own security company, Bulwark Guarding Limited, registered in the UK.

His company, with an active website at bulwarkguarding.co.uk, reflects his entrepreneurial spirit and determination to succeed.

This story captures Yousuf's real-life journey—shaped by his voice and crafted by the author who brought it to the page.

Email: yussuf.Mohammed@gmail.com

About Malick Mahmood

Malick is a passionate storyteller with a background in Film & Television Production from the renowned Film school in New Zealand.

With years of experience as a writer-director for various television channels, he brings a deep understanding of visual narrative, structure, and emotional rhythm to his written work. Over the past two decades, he has authored and co-authored several books across genres—ranging from screenplays and autobiographies to self-help and educational manuals.

For *The Broken Compass*, Malick not only conducted and transcribed extensive interviews but also shaped those raw conversations into a powerful narrative. He so strongly believes in the cinematic power of this story that he has already begun writing a screenplay adaptation.

Malick's books are known for their clarity, sincerity, and impact. He believes in storytelling as a tool for transformation—both for the writer and the reader. He lives by the belief that the right words, at the right time, can change lives.

Email: mahmoodmalick@gmail.com

Printed in Dunstable, United Kingdom